BEN HECHT

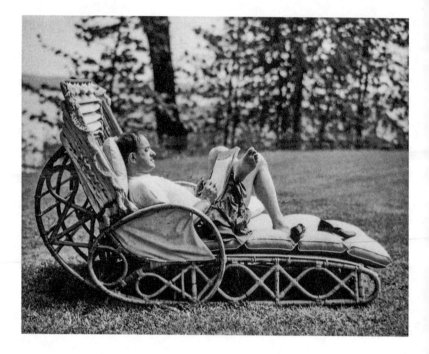

Ben Hecht

Fighting Words,
Moving Pictures

ADINA HOFFMAN

Yale

UNIVERSITY
PRESS
New Haven and London

Frontispiece: Hecht at work, Nyack.

Copyright © 2019 by Adina Hoffman.
All rights reserved.
This book may not be reproduced, in whole or in part, including illustrations, in any form (beyond that copying permitted by Sections 107 and 108 of the U.S. Copyright Law and except by reviewers for the public press), without written permission from the publishers.

Yale University Press books may be purchased in quantity for educational, business, or promotional use. For information, please e-mail sales.press@yale.edu (U.S. office) or sales@yaleup.co.uk (U.K. office).

Set in Janson Oldstyle type by Integrated Publishing Solutions, Grand Rapids, Michigan.
Printed in the United States of America.

Library of Congress Control Number: 2018941583
ISBN 978-0-300-18042-8 (hardcover : alk. paper)

A catalogue record for this book is available from the British Library.

This paper meets the requirements of ANSI/NISO Z39.48-1992 (Permanence of Paper).

10 9 8 7 6 5 4 3 2 1

For Phillip Lopate

"If I could choose of everything I know—I would choose you and Delancey street and myself—but not quite as I am now . . . a different cleverness, an intensity with a bit of Yiddish mooniness in it . . . thirteen kids would be too many . . . I draw the line at four . . . And you railing and laughing at me all day, all night . . . As if we were living long long ago I would prefer that to everything else . . . but when we go back, alas, when someday we walk the ghetto together it will be as misfits—ghetto misfits . . . because we are too many things now to be any one thing perfectly."
—Ben Hecht, from a letter to Rose Caylor, c. 1920

CONTENTS

CONTENTS

BEN HECHT

---◆I◆I◆---

Prologue: The Man

BEN HECHT WAS "a genius," Jean-Luc Godard declared in 1968. "He invented 80 percent of what is used in Hollywood movies today." He "wrote stories—and he made history," proclaimed Menachem Begin four years earlier, at Hecht's standing-room-only Manhattan funeral. When Hecht was still alive, and invariably kicking, Mike Wallace announced on national television that he considered him among "the most disturbing and colorful characters of his time." And as early as 1918, then-London-dwelling Ezra Pound reportedly explained to a friend why he had no desire to return to the American fold. "There is only one intelligent man in the whole United States to talk to"—so the poet is said to have summed up his affection for his homeland—"Ben Hecht."

Hecht called himself a "child of the century," and he was, exuberantly, that. The bad-boy embodiment of much that defined his era, he seemed to know everyone, to be everywhere.

1

Cigar-chomping, wisecracking, Hecht relished the role of brash anti-Zelig—bursting to the front of each new frame and stirring up the action as he flooded the field with his own bold tints.

He was most famous for his scripts. The movies Hecht wrote or cowrote remain among the most delightful ever made, from the silent *Underworld*—for which he won the first-ever Academy Award for best story in 1929—to the vertiginously verbal *Scarface, Nothing Sacred, Gunga Din, Notorious,* and *Twentieth Century,* which, between rounds of Parcheesi and backgammon, he contrived for stage then screen with Charles MacArthur. Another, still more celebrated Broadway comedy by the two former Chicago reporters, *The Front Page,* would become one of the talkiest of the early talkies and later serve as the basis for that giddy marvel of cynical, he-said-she-said newsroom romance, *His Girl Friday.*

Hecht also tinkered in crucial ways with a host of other bona fide classics, including *Gone with the Wind, Foreign Correspondent, Gilda,* and *Roman Holiday.* Counts vary widely: it's estimated that he may have had a hand in as many as 140 films. Pauline Kael credited Hecht with approximately half the entertaining movies to come out of old-time Hollywood and pronounced him "the greatest American screenwriter." Critic Richard Corliss agreed, opening his groundbreaking 1974 survey *Talking Pictures* with the emphatic claim that "Ben Hecht *was* the Hollywood screenwriter." Screwball comedy's airborne patter; the brooding tones of the gangster saga; the newspaper farce and its hard-boiled banter—these were among Hecht's signature modes, and whether or not he fathered these forms, he certainly played a major role in their upbringing.

But scriptwriting was just one of Hecht's occupations—to say nothing of his preoccupations. "There were always a surprising number of me's in operation," he wrote, looking back across his long, slaphappy career, or careers, in journalism, literature, theater, film, and politics. Mercurial as he could be, though, a remarkably unbroken line ran through everything Ben Hecht did. Pugnaciousness and wit figured centrally, as did perversity, a serious sense of play, linguistic dexterity, impatience with decorum and authority. He was also, without fail, prolific. And he did an excellent job of cultivating various legends about himself—so that even now his exploits are most often recounted by means of a hodgepodge of the same salty but well-worn (and not entirely credible) anecdotes, many of his own devising. And while any number of freestanding books might be written about "Hecht's Hollywood" or "Ben Hecht in the Newsroom" or "The Novels of Ben Hecht," all these Hechts were, willy-nilly, one and the same—or variations on a rousing theme—so that attempts to pull apart those strands do little to help us fathom the braid of a man he actually was.

"Ben Hecht the Jew" was also inseparable from these others. Hecht made a point of grandly asserting that he "became a Jew in 1939," when, at age forty-six, he began to "look on the world with Jewish eyes." This account of his own evolution is more than a little absurd, since he had always been Jewish—not *only* Jewish, to be sure (Hecht's Americanness was arguably his true religion), yet bound from birth to that adjective. And here the question of what makes a "Jewish life" seems especially fraught, since he insisted on defining his Jewishness in the narrowest terms, in reaction to Hitler and World War II, as if Germany's invasion of Poland had somehow altered his DNA.

From that date on, Hecht remained, of course, Hecht, though the events of 1939–45 did profoundly change the way he saw himself and how he acted during and after that time. The lessons he drew from this dark period were extreme in a literal sense. They turned him into a Jewish radical, one of the most flamboyant and bellicose boosters of pre-1948 Palestine's militant ultranationalist underground, the Irgun. During these bloody years, he trumpeted his admiration for the "terrorists of Palestine . . . my brave friends," as he called them, in furious response to a world that had, he felt, sat by with criminal passivity as the Nazis slaughtered millions of Jews.

Hecht's crusading wartime work on behalf of those he described as "the doomed Jews of Europe" and his active support for the Irgun were, in the end, as important to him as almost anything. He devotes 110 pages of his memoir to the subject; Hollywood warrants a mere 49. We can question Hecht's grasp of Judaism in general and his own Jewishness in particular (neither was very refined), but the fact remains that he dedicated large chunks of the last several decades of his life to what he considered the "cause." However he did or didn't fathom the complex web of forces that cause entailed—being Jewish was fundamental to being Ben Hecht.

"Oh how dreadfully sad—" Katharine Hepburn scrawled in her rangy, preppy longhand to Hecht's wife, Rose, on hearing the news of his 1964 death, "to have Ben disappear—He seemed as permanent as the Statue of Liberty—"

Disappear he inevitably did, though the speed with which his name has slipped from common memory is striking, given his prominence and/or notoriety at a certain not-too-distant American moment. There are various reasons for this eclipse, some of them understandable, some less so.

Already in 1954, Hecht was musing about his "lack of fame"—a tad disingenuously perhaps, given the acclaim to which he'd been treated for some four decades and the fact that these words appear in a book bound, as he may have predicted, for the best-seller list. He chalked up his wobbly public persona to his self-professed capriciousness. "It is," he wrote, "difficult to praise a novelist or a thinker who keeps popping up as the author of innumerable movie melodramas. It is like writing about the virtues of a preacher who keeps carelessly getting himself arrested in bordellos." If Hecht's claims to present-tense obscurity seem far-fetched, he wasn't wrong about the damage

his casual register-and-discipline hopping had caused his reputation. During his lifetime, all his breezing between art and entertainment, highbrow and low, made him suspect in strictly
literary quarters, and that suspicion followed him past death.
The bordello reference isn't random. The prodigious sums he
earned in Hollywood added to the widespread sense that he had
prostituted his "real" gifts. Never mind that Hecht's screenwriting was vastly better than his fiction. He himself conde-
scended to the movies as a form, and saw scriptwriting as a sort
of verbal whoring, an attitude that surely didn't add to the re-
spect he commanded.

Hecht's onetime idol and sometimes editor H. L. Mencken
articulated rather cruelly the wariness of certain intellectuals
toward Hecht when he wrote late in life that "he had a considerable talent, but there was always something cheap and flashy
about him, so I was not surprised when he gravitated to the
movies." Despite Hecht's well-documented vanity—his creeping baldness dismayed him, he dieted, sucked his gut in for
photos, and for years he worked out with a heavyweight boxer
who visited his house every morning—he seems almost to have
courted such responses, and enjoyed dressing the garish part.
One reporter sketched Hecht as he looked during a 1937 interview: "a stockily built man of medium height, cut something
along the lines of a professional bouncer, with a dark complex-
ion, a stiff mustache and thinning gray-black hair which coils
and wrestles upon his head like a thatch of tangled wire. He was
wearing a wine-colored polo shirt, blue linen trousers and a pair
of yellow buckskin shoes (from his old Hollywood wardrobe,
no doubt), and as he talked the stem of his pipe kept poking in-
differently about the corners of his mouth." The actor George
Jessel described first meeting Hecht at a play rehearsal, where
he'd expected to encounter "a very aesthetic-looking man, the
type that wears a flowing black Windsor tie," and instead found
himself facing the actual Hecht, who sported "a loud red tie and

a shirt that might have been used as a stage curtain for a troupe of very gay midgets."

No matter how vivid Hecht's outfits, the menial status of the "golden age" Hollywood screenwriter also contributed to his more figurative fading out. During the period when Hecht dashed off his sharpest scripts, the movie writer tended to be an almost faceless, backlot presence. Often working in collaboration, on a weekly contract, he (sometimes she) would rush through drafts according to the none-too-profound prescriptions of a bottom-line-minded producer or box-office-fixated studio head. Although Hecht got a good deal more credit than most of his peers—and leveraged that credit, creating what was known as his "script factory," where several other writers joined with him to churn out screenplays under his more bankable name—even *his* movie writing was generally considered glorified hackwork. His vocal disdain for the medium only added to the disappearing-ink quality of his fingerprints on various scripts, as he seemed content to take the money and run, allegedly relieved to be spared the dubious honor of screen credit.

The much-vaunted auteur theory and its lionization of the director as a film's ultimate creator didn't do much to help the memory of a figure like Hecht. While that reductive, romantic approach to reading a movie has been challenged and complicated appreciably since it first came into vogue, the idea that a cinematic work springs whole from the head of a single Zeus-like artist remains lodged in the popular imagination. From TCM to Film Studies 101, Hawks and Hitchcock require no introduction: their last names alone are like superior vintage brands (Cadillac, Chanel). The person responsible for making many of these directors' greatest movies *speak* to us, meanwhile, has been almost forgotten.

Jewish politics, too, probably played a part in the current amnesia surrounding Hecht. Among the first Americans to sound the public alarm about the Holocaust as it was unfolding, and to demand—as he and his small cadre of activist comrades put it—"action, not pity," he seized on a set of maverick (showy, angry, irreverent) consciousness-raising tactics that deeply unsettled the staid American Jewish establishment. The image of Hecht as self-promoting provocateur was one that, in certain circles, stuck. A more damning reading of the contempt heaped on Hecht in such contexts is that his accusations of gross wartime dereliction by America's most powerful Jews—and by the sainted FDR himself—hit much too close to home. The messenger needed to be shot, or at least dismissed as an attention-craving hothead.

Be that as it may, his later swaggering advocacy of violence against the British in Palestine alienated even many of those who applauded his earlier rescue efforts. Ironically enough, though Hecht himself has drifted from view, the state of Israel is now ruled—nearly unchallenged—by those who trace ideological descent from the once-marginal movement he championed.

Whatever the reasons for the blank or confused look Hecht's name now tends to prompt, it's startling to realize the multiple ways in which his life and work still resonate. It's not just that his scripts helped create Hollywood as we know it, or that his raw, gut-felt Irgun "propaganda"—as he unabashedly called it—anticipated the far slicker, more calculating forms of PR that have become commonplace weapons in the rhetorical wars fought over Israel/Palestine. Neither is it merely that Hecht's often brilliant advertisements for himself predicted and even cleared the way for several generations of nervy Jewish-American novelists.

Beyond all these echoes of Hecht's genre-crossing accomplishment, there remains the fact of that label—*Jewish-American*. Well before compound identities were commonplace, when the very idea was cause for severe anxiety (one might, it was often fretted, need to *choose*), Ben Hecht embraced, even celebrated, being an alloy: novelist and journalist, screenwriter and activist, and, perhaps most viscerally, American and Jew, no more, no less. He was—defiantly, unapologetically—a Jewish-American writer, with all the enlivening complication and discomfort that hyphen might imply. "I doubt if there was ever a brighter land than mine," he wrote in 1944 of the United States, as, in almost the same breath, he explained his determination to hold forth in print about Jews, admitting that "the subject is a moody one, and . . . a writer seeking to endear himself had better avoid it." He didn't. But dramatic swings came naturally to Hecht—who, since he was young, had thrilled to the parabolic flight and risk of the artist on his trapeze.

1

The Root

THE STUDIO PORTRAIT snapped in Racine, Wisconsin, 1906,
the year he turned a manly thirteen, shows the oldest son of
Joseph and Sarah (née Swernofsky) Hecht standing still and
proper as could be in his crisply pressed knee breeches. His toes
pointing out like a dancer's in their high-laced patent leather,
he looks every bit the all-American goody-goody. The apparent
tranquility and even obedience of this pose must have pleased
his Russian-born, shtetl-raised parents greatly, but the picture
almost seems an inside joke between the photographer and his
young subject, since as everyone who knew him knew, Bennie
Hecht never stopped moving, plotting, making trouble.

He shot marbles, pistols, arrows tipped with flaming rags.
He sailed a three-foot sloop and a homemade boat six times that
length, its mast patched with canvas scraps he and his friends
cut (stole) at night from awnings along Racine's Main Street.
With the same Ken, Chuck, and Harry, he set potash and tor-

Age thirteen

pedo powder on the town's streetcar tracks; he lit roaring bon-
fires of autumn leaves, manufactured hydrogen in bottles scav-
enged from the city dump, asphyxiated insects and mice in the
same. He played the violin grudgingly in his mother's sitting
room and boisterously in a local saloon; he played a game known
as mumblety-peg. He spun, swung, dangled, and flew on a trapeze, and spent one summer as an apprentice acrobat with a
struggling one-ring circus. He hunted swallows, dug caves, skied
on barrel staves, battled his buddies with sharp tin spears.

His hormones made for further trouble. Writing almost half a century later, he recalled lying and "panting fully clothed atop the best-dressed girl in my class, who would permit no intimacy that involved even the slightest disarrangement of her garments." He also described descending to the basement of his mother's dress shop, in the name of feeding the furnace, then waiting for one—*any* one—of the four female clerks to make her way down to the store's only water faucet, where she would slake her thirst and he would try, clumsily, to grope her. As he grew a bit older and his voice dropped, there were "thunder-clap rendezvous" with various young women, followed by the inevitable "leaping over dark back-yard fences in wild flights from parental wraths."

And when his pulse wasn't racing, his thoughts continued to career as he kept a coded and largely illegible diary of his fumbling sexual exploits (among the few discernible lines: "Life is sin; I wish to live! I must sin!") and tore through book after book after book. He may actually have been as voracious for words as he was for girls—which was saying a very great deal. Never mind the carnelian marbles and dancing skeleton that were among his prized possessions, the most precious item in his boyhood bedroom was a wooden bookcase with leaded glass–paned doors, "a sort of extra continent in the world." He was twelve when the case was lugged up to his gabled attic lair, and while he'd been content then to fill it with boys' books of the Horatio Alger and Oliver Optic variety, the next year, on the same bar mitzvah birthday that occasioned that deceptively static studio shot, a rite of passage was enacted that no synagogue ceremony could rival. That took place when his shy, sweet, barely literate father presented him with four mysterious crates and then retreated downstairs, leaving the boy to discover their contents alone.

Ripping the boards and nails off "like one fallen upon a desert island treasure," Hecht found a rainbow-colored trove of genuine grown-up books—multivolume sets of Shakespeare (maroon with gold titles), Dickens (green), Twain (brick-red), *The World's Famous Orations* (gray), a *History of the World* (blue-back with silver embossing), and something called *The Home Study Circle Library*, whose twenty-five volumes featured excerpts of works by writers from Burns to Byron, Macaulay to Montaigne, as well as miniature biographies of many important dead men. He dove straight into the collected Shakespeare and read late into the nights, his vision blurring. Then, with "an enthusiasm approaching madness," he rampaged through the entire home study set. Even when he lay perfectly still on his bed, one of these thick tomes his only companion, his mind, the words, the world moved so fast they made him dizzy. These sessions left him, he'd later report, "out of breath."

But maybe all Bennie Hecht's restless mental and physical energy was in his Jewish blood. Long before he became a pubescent perpetual motion machine, he and his immigrant family had pulled up and set down stakes multiple times. His parents had arrived in America as teenagers in the mid-1880s—from Minsk or from outside Kremenchug in the Ukraine (Hecht said the latter, his brother the former)—and established themselves in New York's sweatshops. After marrying, Joseph and Sarah climbed the garment district ladder as they moved Bennie (born 1893) and Pete (1897) from Henry Street to Suffolk Street to the far-off realm of the Bronx, eventually setting out with a couple of equally itchy relatives for Boston, then Philadelphia, then Chicago.

By 1903, Joseph had taken to sketching designs for women's suits and coats and hatched a scheme to open a ladies' garment factory in the booming Wisconsin town of Racine, to which he and Sarah and the boys transplanted themselves that year. They rented rooms in a rambling waterfront boardinghouse owned by the widow of a onetime partner of P. T. Barnum and mostly populated by aging circus people. With this graying, sawdust-and-tinsel-minded crew, Ben Hecht's soft-spoken father shared a certain detachment from what might be known, ungenerously, as the real world. According to Ben, Joseph would prove himself a beautiful dreamer and a terrible entrepreneur, for whom "the chief and busiest department of his factory was always an air castle."

Sarah, meanwhile, was vivacious, tough, and far more practical than her husband. After her death, Ben remembered her love of labor. Whether polishing furniture or cooking for hordes of guests, "the expenditure of energy was," in her energetic oldest son's words, "the chief meaning of life for her." But she aspired to more than housework and so invested her own savings in that dress shop, the Paris Fashion, which proved a success. Catering to the more-or-less modish needs of Racine's matrons, the store faced Monument Square, the town's dignified central plaza, named for the imposing Civil War memorial at its heart.

Perched on the shore of Lake Michigan, at the mouth of the Root River, Racine really *was* Middle America at the turn of the twentieth century. With its brick-paved streets and gracious, porch-fronted homes, its stately banks and civic buildings, it seemed to embody everything enterprising the country had accomplished so far and all it aspired to be. Tugboats and coal ships plied its busy harbor. It boasted two railroad depots and factories that churned out floor wax, malted milk, threshing machines. The name Racine comes from the French for "root," and Ben Hecht would in fact trace the roots of his own literary and sensory consciousness to the soil of that wholesome midwestern place, declaring the center of his boyhood various Wordsworth-worthy spots around town.

But there were also earlier, grittier memories that Hecht described later as "ghetto years—young years—dead years whose days are not even ghosts." The tenements, synagogues, barbershops, and fire escapes of the Lower East Side still hovered somewhere in the back corridors of his brain, as did a classroom at the Broome Street School. With a blend of nostalgia and distanced bemusement, he reminisced about, among other wraiths, his grandmother, "whom I hated and in whose kitchen I used to build fires when she wasn't looking in the hopes that the building would burn down and she with it." His grandfather wasn't much more fun, with "his asthma and his interminable Babayaga stories," all of which the old man attributed vaguely to the Talmud. Hecht remembered his father's drugstore hangout near Grand Street and the Yiddish amateur theatrical club in whose plays Joseph Hecht aspired to act but for which instead he always wound up in a much less glamorous role—peddling tickets to his fellow sweatshop cutters.

Ben Hecht's first language was the Yiddish of his parents' home and that teeming ghetto—and its cadences were closely aligned in his mind with a certain broadly rollicking theatricality conjoined with what sounds like a bottomless communal appetite. One early memory unfolded at the Thalia Theater, where Jacob Adler (known as both the Jewish King Lear and a Yiddish-speaking Shylock) starred in *The Kreutzer Sonata*, and "the good folk" of the audience ate chicken throughout the performance. Hecht would also remember how one of his aunts, a Tante Lubi—"her face brightly painted as a rocking horse"— threw herself into organizing benefits for various charities at New York's Yiddish theaters. The performers thronged her apartment after these shows, and there the boy met and marveled at the larger-than-life presence of the great Yiddish actors of the day. Often still outfitted in their tights and tunics, with stage-swords dangling at their sides, Boris Thomashefsky and various greasepainted others came to Lubi's to kick back, play poker, and eat "chiefly out of a huge bowl full of a heavenly food made out of sauerkraut, goose fat and onions all chopped together."

Another aunt, his favorite, Tante Chashe ("tall, swarthy, fat, proud and profane"), was Joseph's sister, married to Sarah's brother. Childless, she had taken to Bennie as if he were her own—much to Sarah's disgust—and during those New York years she showed her adoration by teaching the boy a dozen different card games. While dressed in a nightgown and her husband's slippers, she would play rounds with him for hours on end. She also swept him off regularly to various exhilarating Buffalo Bill–like entertainments and would stretch herself to almost any length to make him happy, at one point cutting down a set of green and gold drapes he'd admired hanging in her rooms and stitching them into an elegant brocade dressing gown for the little prince, a gift.

The bustling Lower East Side and the bucolic Midwest may seem to exist on two separate planets, but in Hecht's sweeping, rich, and at times unabashedly sentimental 1954 memoir, *A Child of the Century*, he conjures a scene that fuses these disparate settings into a single American Jewish pastoral:

The curtain opens onto the crowded back porch of the Racine Hotel on the fourth of July, some steamy summer or other of his boyhood. All his aunts and uncles are present, having magically converged on Sarah and Joseph's town from their far-flung homes in Chicago, New York, and Cleveland. As Hecht scripts the stage directions to this remembered afternoon, they are "drinking beer, roaring with laughter, stripped to their undershirts, and in uncorseted kimonos, and vying with one another in a sort of Yiddish *Canterbury Tales*." Since Racine has no delicatessen of its own, they've come prepared—hauling suitcases filled with smoked white fish, peppered beef, salami, and sour pickles, and they pass much of this particular Independence Day joking, drinking, and noisily eating their delicious, stinky food. After dark, the fireworks over the lakefront flare up, the sky bursts with Roman candles and brilliant skyrockets, and, in what seems a spontaneous celebration of their own hard-won freedom, Ben Hecht's uncles and tantes, his mother and father burst into Yiddish song.

Was this scene fantasy? Reality? ("Memory," Hecht would admit elsewhere, "is the worst of playwrights.") The distinction may not matter as much as does the usually cynical, suddenly misty-eyed middle-aged writer's declaration in the same memoir that he was "in love still with all of them, the dead and the living," and that "it is a love affair that shaped my brain." No matter how far he wandered, this was—*they* were—the place from which he claimed he'd come.

2

The News

BEN HECHT was always falling in love—though he never tumbled harder and faster into that ecstatic state than he did when he met Chicago. "The city of my first manhood," he called it. The place enthralled him with its blur of rooftops and chimneys, its signage and streetcars, its windows, its water, its sky, and especially its crowds. Its crowds! Dashing through downtown, he'd stop suddenly, transfixed, as all those strangers rushed by him on the sidewalk. "I sometimes felt shy," he'd later write of his teenage infatuation with the fact of this great human swirl, "as I stood against a building watching people pass. What if some bright pedestrian saw what I was doing—having a love affair with the faces of the city? It would be hard to explain."

It was July 1910. Having graduated high school in Racine a few weeks earlier and endured exactly three days of summer school at the University of Wisconsin, he'd fled the Madison campus and the prospect of a college degree—hopping a train for the big city and a whole new life. With vague ideas of working as an acrobat, a violinist, or maybe a sailor, he instead wound up bumping into a distant uncle with a red nose, bloodshot eyes, and a more practical plan for his employment. According to the apocryphal-sounding story that Hecht would often repeat, on his first day in Chicago he'd been waiting on line to buy a ticket for a vaudeville matinee when he encountered this only half-remembered relative, a liquor salesman named Manny Moyses. Embarrassed at having been caught playing a very serious sort of hooky—he hadn't yet confessed to his parents that he'd dropped out of college—Hecht felt he had little choice but to follow when his uncle proposed that they call on one of his best booze-buying customers, a Mr. John C. Eastman. Pronouncing his nephew "a hundred-and-twenty-proof genius," Moyses introduced the nervous young Hecht to the publisher of the *Chicago Daily Journal* as "just the thing your great newspaper needs," at which Eastman (also red-nosed) auditioned Hecht on the spot, ordering him to write a dirty poem and promptly leaving for lunch. So the recently graduated chairman of Racine High School's Jest Committee sat for an hour at the desk of the publisher of the oldest Chicago newspaper then in existence and composed six moderately racy verses, complete with an envoi. When Eastman returned, he read the poem, approved, and ushered Hecht into a cavernous space dense with long tables, desks, typewriters, and men in shirtsleeves— some yelling, some sleeping with their hats pulled low over their eyes. He was hired, and told to report at six the next morning to this same spot, which smelled sharply of ink, the paper's local room.

This too was love at first sight.

So many of Hecht's stories about this time and place have the gusty air of legend, it's tempting to count them as sheer make-believe, or at least the vivid hyperbole of a talented teller of tall tales. The fast-talking, heavy-drinking newspapermen who quip and lounge and scheme and bound with such scrappy exuberance across the Criminal Courts Building pressroom stage set of *The Front Page*, the hugely popular 1928 play that Hecht and Charles MacArthur would spin from their experiences as cub reporters in Chicago during these years, seem almost too quick-witted, too hard-boiled to be true. Later in life, though, Hecht would bristle at the charge that he and MacArthur had somehow contrived to "invent a type of newspaper man who never existed." This disbelief was, to Hecht's mind, "sad as well as foolish" and "shows how square the world has grown."

He was being unduly modest. For while Hecht and MacArthur may not have invented this figure from whole cloth, the character really *was* their creation: they lifted him from life and onto the page (then the stage, the screen), and, without exactly concocting him, they stylized him, glamorized him, made him into a hero. By now the hungover reporter in the slouchy fedora with the world-weary worldview and otherworldly way with words has become a kind of sepia-tinged cliché—but when Hecht and MacArthur first set down their valentine to the scruffy denizens of the Chicago newsroom, such a creature did still stroll the city's streets. Others who were present attest to this fact: "citizens who believe . . . [*The Front Page*] to be exaggerated know nothing about the newspaper world of which I am writing," insisted one of Hecht's Chicago colleagues in his own memoir of that uproarious era. And to hear the older Hecht tell it, it was all true. He should know. He'd been one of those hungover hacks: "We were," he'd write with wistful brio, "a tribe of assorted drunkards, poets, burglars, philosophers and boastful ragamuffins. Supermen with soiled collars and holes in our pants, stony broke and sneering at our betters in limousines and unmortgaged houses. Cynical of all things on earth including the tyrannical journal that underpaid and overworked us and for which, after a round of cursing, we were ready to die."

Even in those early days, Hecht felt he'd found his place in the cosmos, though he still needed to scramble up through its celestial ranks. At first, while lodging with his beloved Tante Chashe, he was a lowly picture chaser, assigned to dart across town to one grisly crime scene or another. There he'd finagle a photograph of the day's victim by any means necessary, climbing through windows, jimmying locks, blocking a chimney in order to smoke a grieving family out of its home and so snatch a framed portrait of the recently murdered, raped, or maimed from a sideboard or mantle. He would generally wind up his journalistic breaking-and-entering by midmorning and so had plenty of time on his hands, which is why at some point he was ordered to keep busy by finding a story to write. This he did, happily, and to great acclaim in the local room—though that act marked, as he would admit with a certain overly alliterative pride, his "sudden fearless flowering as a fictioneer." Which is to say that while he may not have invented the swashbuckling newsmen who populated *The Front Page*, he completely fabricated these first stories he "reported." He and a photographer sidekick even conspired to stage shots to accompany these made-up scoops—pictures of the brave tugboat captain who'd allegedly fended off pirates on Lake Michigan and images of the devastation wrought by the severe earthquake that was said to have rocked Chicago. In order to capture on film this putative tremor's aftermath, they'd spent several hours on the Lincoln Park beach digging a yawning trench.

The truth—or, more accurately, his bosses at the paper—eventually caught up with him. Hecht was scolded but forgiven these outlandish flights of tabloid fancy, and with time, he evolved into a more fact-checkable sort of reporter, becoming a protégé of sports editor Sherman Duffy, who read Latin, French, and Spanish, smoked a pipe, dangled his Phi Beta Kappa key from his vest pocket, bred irises, and could drink any man under the city desk. Duffy taught his eager apprentice critical lessons about what and how to write: "Never get too fancy," Duffy instructed. "Be sure your style is so honest that you can put the word shit in any sentence without fear of consequences." After work, Hecht would trail Duffy around the neighborhood saloons, absorbing in silent wonder the witty, raunchy banter of his mentor and his whiskey-loving pals—columnists, critics, sports promoters, grizzled veterans of the wire services and Hearst papers. And it seems he learned as much about language from these barroom sessions as he did from all his reading: "The whiplash phrase, the flashing and explosive sentence, the sonorous syntax and bull's eye epithet" of these drunken outings were, according to Hecht, "the great event . . . of my first years as a newspaperman." Who needed journalism school?

Now Hecht was assigned more substantive stories—covering floods and funerals, trials and hangings. He specialized in crime and corruption in their most sensational forms, but he also interviewed everyone from William Jennings Bryan to Freudian fetish expert Wilhelm Stekel to the Yiddish poet Morris Rosenfeld. ("I am an American first and a Jew afterward," Hecht quoted Rosenfeld in a 1913 article, "and the Jewish future I think lies in the future of this country, not of Palestine. What do you think, am I wrong?") As he became the paper's star reporter, he also continued to hang around Duffy's office, typing up box scores, schmoozing, and learning a few important things about how low and high might meet in the workplace—or, really, anywhere. On one occasion, between innings of the ballgame they were reporting from a wire account, he converted into elegant rhymed verse a prose translation of Apuleius's *Golden Ass* that Duffy had just rendered, banging it out at the same furious rate as the baseball play-by-play.

After a brief stint renting a room with another reporter on the fourth floor of a grand North Dearborn Street mansion that turned out to be the city's most notorious bordello, he moved in with his parents, who had given up the Racine dress shop and followed him to Chicago. Although by this stage he had abandoned the fabrication of dramatic news stories, he'd recently found another outlet for his urge to fictionalize and, at night, in secret, begun to write novels and short stories. And promptly to burn them. This urge to incinerate his handiwork welled up not from the belief that what he'd written was *bad*—but because it was complete. He wrote, he insisted, not out of ambition but from the sheer delight that swept him when words accumulated on the page. (It took time to understand this as a kind of narcissism that "finds pleasure in staring into the contents of one's own head.") He also continued to read like a fiend, and spent most of his small paycheck on books.

Among the newspapermen of Chicago in the 1910s, Hecht was hardly unique in what he called his "book hunger." He and his journalist friends devoured work by Proust and Pushkin, Nietzsche and Tolstoy, and argued about free verse. Neither did his own nascent literary attempts distinguish him in this context. Every copyboy and city editor was, it seems, scribbling poems or novels on the side—and they weren't just dabbling. After Hecht accepted a higher paying job at the *Chicago Daily News* in 1914, he recommended that his new boss, the refined Henry Justin Smith—himself a scholar of Greek and an aspiring novelist—hire a fine reporter named Carl Sandburg, whom Hecht had met recently in the pressroom at the Criminal Courts Building, and who also happened to write poetry. Hecht and Sandburg would become confidants, as they worked at adjacent desks at the *News* for years and took long walks around Sandburg's City of the Big Shoulders, just around the time the poet was famously characterizing it as such. Sandburg had the finest voice Hecht had ever heard, laced with a certain mystery and freshness: "He spoke always," wrote Hecht, "like a man slowly revealing something." One of those things Sandburg would re-

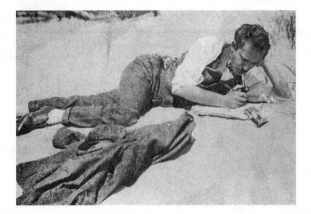

. . . a living scrawl, a writhing writ . . .

veal was his view of Hecht in these years. In an unpublished poem from this period, "Sketches for Cartoon of Ben Hecht," he conjures "Books on his desk and books in his pockets./People on the streets and people in houses./These he reads, these the books, these the people./They write a living scrawl, a writhing writ . . ." This goes on for a very Sandburgian page and a half and ends with a cryptic though striking: "He takes an old mouth organ,/and goes away down our Mississippi nocturns,/a Jewish Huck Finn . . . alone."

That solitary (and Semitic) image may say something true about who Hecht really was, deep down or late at night as he wrote and burned his first attempts at fiction, but in actuality, most of his hours during these years were crowded with all kinds of people—coworkers, drinking buddies, and conversational companions (mostly men), as well as various women. During this same period he lived briefly in an attic room overlooking the river with a fresh-faced prostitute he was trying— and failing—to reform, and he met a well-bred "girl reporter," Marie Armstrong, who came from an upstanding Episcopalian family from the suburb of Highland Park. Softly pretty Marie impressed Hecht immediately with the French books she was always reading, with the green-inked ribbon she used to type her stories—and with the fact of her so-called virtue. He had, he confessed, never "consorted with a 'good woman,'" and the idea seemed to excite him.

As he filed copy, caroused, and courted the virtuous Miss Armstrong, Hecht also plunged into another charmed Chicago realm, one whose heady atmosphere and comically accomplished cast of characters would, with time, affect him as much as the newsroom and its boys-will-be-boys antics. Entrée into this magical kingdom began with attendance at a salon that took place weekly at the studio of a woman named Margery Currey, the *Daily News*'s resident "sob sister," and until recently a schoolteacher, suffragette, and the wife of socialist editor and novelist Floyd Dell. Currey and Dell had first hosted these evenings together, and though the tradition had kicked off casually enough, their gatherings gradually emerged as a major catalyst for what would come to be known in textbook terms as the Chicago Renaissance—though it's worth keeping in mind how such cultural flowerings look in real time. As one witness to the events points out, "The Chicago Literary Renaissance was occurring; but none of the participators in it knew about it." After the couple separated, Currey continued to throw these free-form soirées, inviting various friends and acquaintances to take the hourlong streetcar ride from downtown out to 57th Street and Stony Island Avenue, where a ragtag artist's colony had sprung up in the abandoned storefronts left behind after the 1893 World's Fair. Former restaurants, shops, photo studios, these tumbledown, one-story buildings were now populated by a scramble of writers, painters, craftsmen, and thinkers—Thorstein Veblen had theorized about conspicuous consumption there—and Currey's converted Chinese laundry was the buzzing hub of the bohemian enclave.

At her parties, tall candles flickered as guests dug into a

communal pail of chop suey and drank cheap wine, read their work aloud, argued, and talked late into the night. Theodore Dreiser was often there, as were Edgar Lee Masters and Sand- burg. Hecht himself became a regular at Currey's shindigs, where he could usually be found immersed in tipsy conversa- tion with, among many others, two writers—Swatty and Bogie, as he called them—who would matter to him deeply over the years, sometimes as dear friends, sometimes as sworn enemies. The two were equally unpublished and unfamous when he came to know them, though their literary and personal lives would soon swerve in very different directions and represent for Hecht two polar extremes—cautionary tales of how an American writ- er's life might unfold, in the brightest spotlight or the darkest shadows. And what kind of writer would *he* be?

Currey had first dragged Hecht to meet Swatty at the Cass Street rooming house where he then lived. Hecht had been re- luctant to go to a party hosted by a stranger he knew of as "an Advertising Man," but the gathering proved more surprising than the dull affair he'd expected. After drinking gin from a water glass and talking to this one and that one—*Poetry* maga- zine's formidable founder and editor Harriet Monroe was there, as were various South Side poets, English painters, and Russian intellectuals—he settled into a spot on the floor, things quieted down, and Swatty, a.k.a. Sherwood Anderson, began to intone one of the stories he'd recently written about a town he called Winesburg, Ohio.

Though the stories seemed to Hecht "very mystic and a little illiterate," and he thought Anderson excessively pleased with Anderson—he read aloud as though he were a preacher offering revelations of the God who was . . . himself—Hecht would quickly come around and emerge as a devoted and gen- erous advocate, pushing editors to publish the older writer's work, issuing strong reviews when it appeared between covers, and later dubbing Anderson "our genius . . . our Renaissance,

With Sherwood Anderson

our Daniel Boone of Art. . . . It was," he wrote, "Sherwood who reinvented the American soul." The two grew close and even set out to write a play together about Benvenuto Cellini—an effort they abandoned after the first act swelled to a hundred and twenty pages, which Hecht thought far too long and Anderson deemed not quite long enough. Dismissing the editorial suggestions of his younger but more experienced collaborator (Hecht had recently been writing what he described as "sane and practical little plays" together with a wealthy Princeton graduate named Kenneth Sawyer Goodman), Anderson insisted that "people who went to the theater were all pernicious idlers and would be grateful for a drama that ran eight hours."

The middle-aged copywriter and the boyish newspaperman were very different in temperament and bearing. Anderson often indulged in flights of vatic musing, or what Hecht dubbed "owlish words." Hecht was a much more grounded, restless, and skeptical sort of wise guy. Anderson ribbed him and called him a "Newspaper Ned," blind to life's truths. But they also shared a few essential characteristics: Hecht felt himself drawn to Anderson's "compelling salesmanship," something people often said of him. Hecht questioned the truthfulness of the stories Anderson told about himself—as he was occasionally questioned about the truth of the stories *he* told about *himself.* They were both seducers by nature, both basically indifferent to critical opinion, and both known for a quicksilver sort of charm that could, and now and then did, erupt into flashes of anger.

After Hecht included a barely masked portrait of Anderson in his first novel, the obviously autobiographical 1921 *Erik Dorn,* Anderson was enraged and, according to Hecht, offered him a deal over lunch one day: they'd been friends for some seven years, which was—as Anderson-as-quoted-by-Hecht put it—"a long time. . . . It kind of wears off and loses its point, friendship does. My idea is that we become enemies from now on. Real enemies. You do everything you can to injure me. Attack me, denounce me, try to steal my girls, ravish my wife—anything you want. And I'll do the same to you. That way we can have a lot of fun—instead of just piddling along as a couple of fellows getting more and more bored with each other." Anderson himself never wrote of such a strange conversation, and in his own memoirs—filtered through the forgiving scrim of his later acclaim—he describes with apparent pleasure tagging along with Hecht when he covered news stories. In this milder account of their relationship, "we quarreled and fought, made up, remained friends," though in a trenchant, undated, and presumably more reliable letter that appears in Anderson's archive, he expresses his irritation—and bedrock identification—with the younger man. This is hardly the declaration of war Hecht describes but seems instead a kind of white flag—albeit one hoisted as pointed rebuke: "Just for a kind of vacation consider, just for a moment that you aren't as highly specialized a thing as you think," Anderson dares Hecht. "You and I for example are friends. Try the experiment of saying to yourself that there isn't any smart thoughts I may have that Anderson may not have too, there isn't any love I have so deep that Anderson may have had one just as deep . . . The bluff you throw about being so full of energy and being so smart and fast dont bluff me. I've got your number on that because you're so very like myself. . . . It is a fact that every time I am with you I feel your liking me OK but at the same time I feel antagonism. Lets disarm. There aren't such a hell of a lot of people a man can talk to. If I am like another side to you perhaps you are like another side to me too."

As these two were circling each other, Hecht was also growing close to—and dueling dramatically with—another, still more pugnacious writer he'd met that same evening when he'd reluctantly followed Marjy Currey to Anderson's Cass Street rooming house. This was "Bogie," who struck Hecht then as "a slim, golden-haired youth with pale blue eyes and the pensive face of Christ in the [Heinrich] Hofmann painting. . . . A soiled and bulging brief case was under one arm. In the other hand he held a corncob pipe in which a foul tobacco . . . smoldered and reeked."

"Are you prepared to listen to the exquisite prose of our host?" Hecht remembered him asking. "Or would you prefer the briefer torture of one of my sonnets?" Maxwell Bodenheim tended to speak in these wryly overwrought terms, which weren't far from the purple way he wrote. Born Maxwell Bodenheimer,

Maxwell Bodenheim

the flamboyantly self-destructive poet, novelist, paranoiac, drunk, beggar, and, in his own almost-proud terminology, "black-guard" would become, for Hecht, "one of the great conversers of my youth." Decades later, Hecht chalked this up to the fact that "we shared a common set of disdains and were equally de-voted to adjectives," though the bond was actually much more complex, and poignant, than that. With his violent temper, searing cynicism, contempt for authority, capacity for linguis-tic gymnastics, and, just behind these many masks, a throbbing sort of vulnerability, the defiantly undomesticated Bodenheim was a fun-house mirror reflection of the far suaver, saner, and less needy Hecht—a grotesquely distorted version of what Hecht might have been, had he let himself run wild. In a pa-rodic though shrewdly insightful portrait of Bodenheim that Hecht offered up during these years, he describes his snarling, gap-toothed friend as having "the air of a kaleidoscopic moun-tebank." He might have been describing himself on certain mornings.

It is perhaps also worth noting that Bodenheim, like Hecht,

was Jewish. The son of a successful dry goods merchant who had moved to southern Mississippi from Alsace-Lorraine, he had been jailed while serving in the U.S. Army in Texas, after a lieutenant "ridicule[ed] Private Bodenheim as a Jew" and he promptly beaned his superior over the head with a musket. Hecht and Bogie were the only Jewish members of the loosely defined group that converged to drink and plot artistic revolution at Marjy Currey's or in Anderson's Cass Street room—a fact that wouldn't necessarily mean much, except that it seems to have contributed to the sense around town that the two had, as one genteelly WASPy commentator put it, "early adopted the pose of a friendly enmity between themselves," borrowing their tricks from "Montague Glass and his comical pair, Potash and Perlmutter." Was it a Jewish conspiracy? To call this anti-Semitism would be too strong, though the slightly acrid scent of Christian condescension wafts over the words of this critic, who explains that neither Hecht nor Bodenheim was "exactly of the ghetto, yet there flamed in each of them that intensity which the ghetto hands down to its posterity, even to those remote from its awry gates." Pointing to "this intensity bordering on nervousness," he does credit them with being "the most colorful figures of Chicago's bohemia of 1913–1923." While others might have produced greater work—Sandburg, Anderson, Masters—he acknowledges that the duo of Bodenheim and Hecht provided the "action, scandal, amours. They were the unlaced souls of the group, the starters of clubs and journals, the noisy bearers of flags."

But was that really all? In fact, both men aspired to make a good deal more than noise.

A serious hunger for serious art also drove them. And in these same years Hecht would find a critical source of sustenance and encouragement for his own art—not from another combative male friend or foil, but from a strikingly poised young woman who came into his life at this time and who was, in the words of Hecht's possibly jealous then-girlfriend, Marie Armstrong, "the nurse of his earliest talents." He would not be "the genius" he had become, Marie would write, "but for the straining, unearthly, hectic fires of her enthusiasm for him." And Ben Hecht wasn't alone: the fires of her enthusiasm lit up in spectacular fashion the whole horizon of contemporary letters.

One evening, in the summer of 1913, this high-minded and highly enterprising twenty-one-year-old Indiana transplant put in an appearance at Currey's salon, as she often did. For several weeks now, she'd been telling everyone she knew that she was "about to publish the most interesting magazine that had ever been launched." But—as she announced to the company assembled around the chop suey pail that night—she needed a title. They batted around possible names—*The Unicorn? The March Review? The Eagle's Feather? Pen and Ink?* None seemed quite right. She herself was toying with *The Seagull* ("soaring," as she'd later write, "and all that kind of thing"). In the end she settled on *The Little Review*—which sounded straight, simple, and diminutive enough, though the magazine she would start publishing that March was anything but.

In middle age, Hecht would declare that Margaret Anderson—no relation to Sherwood—had been for him in those early days "Keeper of the Literary Heavens." Her magazine had remained in his mind since that time, he wrote, "a piece of the True Cross, glimpsed by a pilgrim in his youth. It was," he proclaimed, with a certain rueful, backward-looking awareness, perhaps, of all that to which he felt he *hadn't* devoted himself later in life, "Art . . . nakedly and innocently, Art." Hecht may have been the great hyperbolizer, but in fact *The Little Review* was really that—nothing less than the launch pad for literary modernism in America. Propelled by Anderson's preternaturally sensitive literary taste buds, her prodigious editorial imagination, and her sheer nerve, the magazine published in the

course of just a few years enough major work by enough soon-
to-be major writers to fill a whole century's worth of English
Department syllabi. Before their names were widely known,
James Joyce, Ezra Pound, William Carlos Williams, William
Butler Yeats, Gertrude Stein, T. S. Eliot, Ford Madox Ford,
Wyndham Lewis, Djuna Barnes, André Gide, Jean Cocteau,
and numerous only slightly less illustrious others appeared side
by side on the pages of her journal. She often found herself
in—or threw herself into—hot water, as when her outspoken
support for Emma Goldman and the anarchist cause led to the
journal's eviction from its office, or when she serialized Joyce's
Ulysses. That act famously brought about the confiscation and
incineration of several issues of *The Little Review* by the postal
authorities; it also landed Anderson and her partner in life and
work, Jane Heap, in a New York City courtroom, where they
were convicted of obscenity.

But all that would come later—after Anderson and Heap
had joined forces with Pound, as foreign editor, and relocated to
Greenwich Village. When the twenty-two-year-old Ben Hecht
first came to know Anderson, in the minuscule office she'd
rented for the magazine on the eighth floor of the Fine Arts
Building on Chicago's Michigan Avenue, she was just getting
her literary bearings, though she'd already fixed her eye on a
very big prize: "Life," she announced in the first issue, "is a
glorious performance . . . And close to Life—so close, from
our point of view, that it keeps treading on Life's heels—is this
eager, panting Art, who shows us the wonder of the way as we
rush along." As was his wont, he fell a bit in love with her, and
though chic, blonde Anderson was impervious to Hecht's romantic advances (she was both busy with loftier things and a
lesbian), he was known to be her favorite—even a kind of pet.
From the moment his work first appeared in the magazine in
May 1915, his name would be prominently featured in almost
every issue for several exhilarating years.

"I remember its beginning and my own beginnings as almost identical," he would write of *The Little Review*, and as Anderson was finding her editorial way, Hecht was grasping to figure out who he was as a writer. She gave him a platform, and he jumped up onto it. These early efforts—criticism, poetry, satirical social commentary—are often grossly overwritten and fixated on an adolescent need to *épater le bourgeois;* some of what he published (the poetry in particular) is just awful. But there were flickers here of what he was capable of. Whether marveling at the "staggering effects" of Dostoevsky's *The House of the Dead* or inveighing against the "Slobberdom, Sneerdom, and Boredom" he experienced at a stuff-shirted exercise known as a Walt Whitman dinner ("When one hears that a Walt Whitman dinner is to be given on a certain night in the Grand Pacific Hotel all one has to do to remain happy and free from suffering is to stay at home"), Hecht was positioning himself, elatedly, as both celebrator *and* scold, applying the verbal lessons he'd learned from Sherman Duffy and his talkative barroom buddies, while stretching himself intellectually to write about something more lasting than the morning's news. As he tested his talents, he was also testing the limits, seeing how far he could go in print and/or what he could get away with in life. So it was that in the magazine's lead essay of August 1915, he skewered the stifling conformity and pretensions of a prototypical middle-class, middlebrow American family, "which considers culture a matter of polished fingernails and emotional suppression and dinner table aphorisms, puns and the classics in half morocco." That this portrait was based very plainly, and aggressively, on the family of his girlfriend, the virtuous Marie, caused a crisis between them—with her parents forbidding her ever to see him again.

While it may have been the first time he'd used his writing as a weapon, it was hardly the last. And it wasn't the final time that his words caused pain. Years afterward, with a great deal of muddy water under the bridge between them, Marie would accuse "the genius" of having been "outraged because my parents did not instantly admire and worship him." Before this crisis, her father had pronounced Hecht "a smart-Aleck kid, clever enough and probably a good writer—but I don't like him." And now, to exacerbate matters, Hecht had, according to Marie, written "a vituperative, vicious essay against such hopeless souls as were 'Anglo-Saxon, normal and nice.'" Nasty as his lampoon was, her account of his essay also stings a little. Though he didn't go out of his way to call attention to it, Hecht's religion seemed often to be lurking somewhere in the background of these questionable character assessments. "He did not look especially Jewish in those days" was the older if not necessarily wiser Marie's curious account of how Hecht had seemed to her then. And much as she'd loved him, she found his "attitude toward his race . . . baffling." As she explains, "among the hundreds of letters I received from him was one that particularly pleased my mother. [Ben] had written about my parents' objections to him. He added that he did not emphasize the fact that he was a Jew, because he 'did not wish to boast.' In spite of her dislike for him, this phrase stuck in mother's memory, and she often quoted it with admiration."

For all the arrogance and even cruelty he unleashed in "The American Family," Hecht could also write far more earnestly, as he showed with his first published fiction, which appeared in the November 1915 issue of *The Little Review*. In these crude but compelling stories, grouped together as "Dregs," the main character, Moisse, "the young dramatist," wanders around Chicago's Jewish ghetto and beyond it, registering the filthy alleys, children pissing in the gutter, an old man whose beard swarms with lice, desperate beggars, and simpering whores of both sexes. As Hecht veers in and out of repulsion, fascination, and sympathy, he also presents an intriguing self-portrait, which swings

The young dramatist, c. 1918

between mockery and pride. He seems to know how pretentious Moisse is: to call him "the young dramatist" implies that. The main thing the character is dramatizing is himself. But for all the adolescent cockiness that comes with his musing that, for example, "I am the only one in the street whose soul is awake," Moisse appears also to be aware of the responsibility that comes with such heightened perception. He refuses to look away from the wretchedness he's seeing, and feels obliged to record every detail, not to flinch.

The response to the stories was strong and swift, with some readers writing Anderson to praise Hecht's work and others to cancel their subscriptions: "LITTLE REVIEW—how *could* you do it?" one horrified reader demanded to know. "You who have hitherto held so bravely to the tenets of beauty and truth in thought and expression . . . consent to print descriptions of the bestial abnormalities of the scum of mankind!" while another sent on a simple "Good stuff, Ben Hecht!" Anderson, for her part, defended "Dregs" in the firmest terms, declaring the stories "among the best things *The Little Review* has printed." (Apparently enjoying his newfound ability to shock, Hecht soon recycled the title *Dregs* to stir up wider controversy with a one-act play. Starring Bodenheim as a drunk who mistakes his own reflection in a barroom window for the face of Christ, this raw piece of underground theater was denounced by the drama critic of the *Chicago Tribune* for the "unbelievable squalor of [its] words" and generally considered blasphemous. It closed after a few performances, though it added to Hecht's growing notoriety.)

The same month that his first stories appeared, Hecht and Marie were married. Despite her parents' objections and her own hurt feelings, they had reconciled in secret, and when her father died suddenly in October, they sprang into action, scrambling to find an Episcopal priest to do the honors. Moving into a four-room apartment on the South Side, they bought a grand piano on an installment plan and settled in; soon Marie was pregnant. By the time their daughter, Edwina (they'd call her Teddy), was born the next November, the Hechts had moved into an eight-room apartment that Marie began furnishing in high style and well beyond their modest means.

Still working at the *Daily News* for forty dollars a week, Hecht was now the head of a well-appointed bourgeois household that was not so very different from the one he had recently and viciously mocked in print. They'd soon have a cook, two servants, and several thousand dollars' worth of debt. It was ostensibly because of this debt—or, more immediately, an

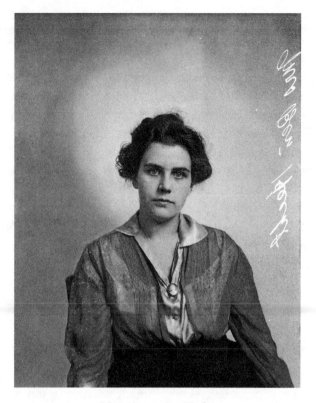

Marie Armstrong Hecht

angry butcher who had arrived in their kitchen on the eve of
one of Marie's dinner parties, demanding immediate payment
of the three hundred dollars they owed him—that Hecht took
the next, fateful step of his writing career. That very evening
he retreated to his study, sat down at his typewriter, and, after
two hours, tucked the manuscript of what he called his "first
commercial story" into an envelope and sent it to the Mid-
town Manhattan address of *The Smart Set*, attention: H. L.
Mencken.

Six days later, the mailman arrived, bearing a check for
forty-five dollars and an acceptance letter, signed "Yours in

Christ" by the great contrarian critic and editor himself. It was just the first of numerous stories and plays that Hecht would publish in the monthly, which billed itself A MAGAZINE OF CLEVERNESS and which seemed, on its glossy surface, the exact opposite of *The Little Review*. With its bright drawing of a flirty girl on the cover each month, its ads for Bromo-Seltzer, Hyglo Nail Polish, and the Breakers Hotel in Atlantic City, *The Smart Set* appeared a far and fast-paced cry from Margaret Anderson's journal, with its restrained monochrome jackets and airborne aspirations. While *The Little Review* had recently adopted as its own motto MAKING NO COMPROMISE WITH THE POPULAR TASTE, *The Smart Set* was an unapologetically commercial affair, aimed at a wide audience, its table of contents chockablock with perky "Bicycle Built for Two"–like titles such as "There Are Two Little Ladies in Our Town" and "To Please Penelope." Anderson couldn't afford to pay her writers, hoping that service to the cause of Art would be recompense enough; Mencken and his coeditor George Jean Nathan, meanwhile, ran their magazine as a matter-of-fact business, based principally, in Mencken's words, "on a civilized skepticism," as well as "adroit and colorful writing." A civilized skeptic himself, the debt-strapped Hecht was happy to earn money by cranking out such adroit and colorful work. His journalistic experience had prepared him well for this brisk tack, and he wrote quickly and easily in this mode, sometimes using a pseudonym and even dashing out fiction according to the irony-rich plots fed to him by Mencken. "Write a story," the editor would demand, "about a young Mormon in Utah who falls so deeply in love with a young woman that he refuses to wed and take into his bed the three more wives prescribed by the Mormon Gospel of that time. And so he flees with his one wife and lives in sinful monogamy with her, in St. Louis."

Despite Hecht's financial explanation for his decision to start tossing off fiction for *The Smart Set*, money wasn't the only reason for his turn in this direction. Mencken had long been a hero of his—he referred to the "H. L. Mencken tuning fork" that "awoke the iconoclast in me"—and in many ways, the wars Mencken was fighting were also Hecht's wars, against hypocrisy, cant, and pussyfooting. Stylistically, temperamentally, the two had a great deal in common. Mencken "waded into . . . battle," wrote Hecht, ". . . not like a philosopher in a frock coat but like a barroom brawler with his shirt sleeves up." He was, in Hecht's estimation, "after the soul of the Republic, sunk to its intellectual knees and kissing the rump of every platitude on the calendar."

And for all the avant-garde elitism of *The Little Review* and the splashy populism of *The Smart Set*, the two journals were not quite as different as they seemed at first glance. They both aimed to vanquish common enemies (middlebrows, closed minds), and even published some of the same writers. *The Little Review* had, it's true, a much higher batting average when it came to discovering lasting work, but scattered among its many forgettable contributions, *The Smart Set* featured, over the years, stories and plays by Joseph Conrad, D. H. Lawrence, Theodore Dreiser, Sherwood Anderson, Sinclair Lewis, and the young F. Scott Fitzgerald. Like *The Little Review*, it too championed Pound and Joyce; several of the *Dubliners* stories made their first American appearance on its pages (though no-nonsense Mencken had little patience with *Ulysses*, which he called "deliberately mystifying and mainly puerile").

Hecht's work for Mencken was certainly derivative and sometimes had the quality of a sardonic one-liner. But here was the dirty secret: it was also consistently livelier, sharper, more controlled, and less strained than the often heavy-handed imitations of various American naturalists and European decadents he was now laboring to produce for Margaret Anderson. Not everyone, though, thought so, and in fact Hecht's knack for breezy humor seems to have troubled those who would have preferred he stick to a single mode, and to more serious matters. The new foreign editor of *The Little Review*, Ezra Pound, for instance, admired Hecht but was impatient with his cleverness, writing Anderson in early 1918 that "Hecht might write good DeMaupassant if he didn't try to crack jokes and ring bells," and declaring a few months later that "Hecht is an asset . . . When he gets out of his head the idea that he must suit S. Set public . . ., he CAN write . . . i.e. can, (future tense) (will be able to)." Hecht himself, meanwhile, was hoping he could (present tense) manage to do at least two things at once— produce art at the highest level *and* whip off fizzy yet biting entertainments whose proto–screwball comedy characters all had names like Hazel Wombat, Miama Gimmel, Ballad Mac- Arthur, and the Rev. Lloyd Blop.

3

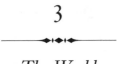

The World

HE HAD A KNACK for finding himself right in the thick of it, whatever, wherever *it* was. And now, after dark on December 30, 1918, there he was at the Hotel Adlon, Berlin, the snow falling softly outside.

What happened exactly that night? Hecht was a chronic recycler—and drastic reviser—of the autobiographical anecdote, a kind of one-man *Rashomon*, and as his early ventures into bogus news stories make clear, he wasn't beyond pure fabrication. (As Norman Mailer would frame it many years later, Hecht was "never a writer to tell the truth when a concoction could put life in his prose.") In one account of what took place that chilly German evening just weeks after the end of the First World War, he sat in the dining room of the grand hotel on Unter den Linden. As he finished his solitary dinner of blue-ish potatoes, bluefish, and cheese, the waiter whispered a tip: Karl Liebknecht, comrade of Rosa Luxemburg and leader of the revolutionary Spartacus League, was plotting to attack the kaiser's palace that very night. The twenty-five-year-old Hecht had just arrived in Germany that afternoon, as foreign correspondent for the *Chicago Daily News*, and though he'd never heard of Liebknecht—he spoke no German and knew "as little about European politics as it was possible for an American newspaperman to know"—he recognized a scoop when it came his way, and within a few hours had penetrated the inner sanctum of the recently abdicated emperor's residence, watching as Liebknecht cried out rousing slogans about freedom and the proletariat, then stripped down to his tattered long underwear and, guarded by a hundred well-armed marines in matching pancake hats, climbed into the kaiser's bed.

It was snowing and dark in another Hechtian version of the night's doings, though in this variation, he was alone in his room at the Hotel Adlon, listening to the sound of gunfire in the distance when the phone rang and announced the arrival in the lobby of one Carl von Doehmann, a German poet and doctor Hecht had met on the train from Amsterdam the day before. Doehmann dismissed Hecht's questions about the revolution then possibly erupting outside—"in reality," Doehmann assured him, "it was only a few more corpses being piled up around the altar of nonsense"—and, promising him a more interesting lead, whisked him off in a droshky to go meet "the greatest man in Germany," a young artist named George Grosz.

What, again, really happened that night? In Grosz's own memoirs, he recalls his first meeting with Hecht as having taken place at some later date. Then the same Herr Doktor Doehmann—known in their Dadaist circle as Daimonides, a wild improviser of music and author of grotesque verse—took Grosz along to a party that had sprung up at the Adlon. The host, "whom everyone called Benny," was playing "Everybody Shimmies Now" on the violin. His wife accompanied him at the piano, on top of which the fun-loving American fiddler sat

Inhaber:

Ben Hecht
(Chicago Daily News)
(Stand, Vor- und Zuname)

wohnhaft in

Berlin N.W. Unter den Linden

Hotel Adlon

(Ort, Straße, Hausnummer)

Press pass, Berlin, 1919

cross-legged, surrounded by overflowing ashtrays and half-empty liquor bottles.

However contradictory these scenarios, a few facts about the events that unfolded in and around the Adlon that winter are verifiable. That Ben Hecht and George Grosz became life-long friends is corroborated by the books on which they worked together over the years and by Hecht's archive, which brims with affectionate letters, doodled in the German caricaturist's playful hand. Hecht's telegraphic dispatches and published newspaper articles, a photo album lovingly compiled by Marie Armstrong Hecht, and correspondence that dates from the charged months that he (and indeed she, absent from his own retrospective accounts) spent in Berlin also confirm a more basic truth—

that Hecht wasn't exaggerating when he looked back across some three and a half decades and declared this "the most dramatic time I had yet lived."

The Hechts were among the first Americans to arrive in Germany after the war. Having put their fine furniture in Chicago storage, deposited two-year-old Teddy with Marie's mother, and stopped in London, where they visited Ezra Pound and ate lunch with Wyndham Lewis, they must have known they were in for a major adventure. But even the highly imaginative Ben Hecht couldn't have foreseen all the real-life theatrics to which they'd be spectators and that he would report to the world. "Weimar. February fifth," reads one typical 1919 telegraphic dispatch, "The narrow meandering streets old Weimar witnessed today opening germanys most desperate battle stop strange men in silk hats frock coats came hurrying into little byways sacred to memories Goethe Schiller Luther stop little merchants and stolid farmers from bavaria saxony comma financiers labor leaders from silesia dash a wonderful conglomeration students agitators politicians peasants came pouring into dreaming city of german muses to work out salvation of idle starving bankrupt conquered seventy million people stop." Within weeks, fighting in the Berlin streets between the socialist government's troops and the Spartacist revolutionaries raged, and one afternoon the Hechts' taxicab was attacked by an armed mob. Days later Hecht saw from behind a cathedral pillar the peaceful surrender of thousands of Spartacists to the army at Alexanderplatz. Despite the nonviolent actions of the crowd, he soon found himself climbing a tree just outside the jail where many of the same revolutionaries were being held for treason and where, with a pair of field glasses, he witnessed the grisly episode that he'd rush to write up as soon as he climbed down: "All morning I have watched soldiers and workingmen being marched handcuffed through the streets under heavy guard of troops with machine guns to the wall of Moabit prison, there to be executed." In a matter of hours, Hecht wrote, hundreds (he later claimed thousands) were slaughtered, and when his story appeared in papers across Europe and America after a few days, he was commanded to leave Germany by midnight, "for reporting lies." Instead he would remain, and the massacre would become widely known, as would the murders of Liebknecht and Luxemburg, who were both beaten with rifle butts, then shot dead, his body dumped in the Tiergarten park, hers in the Landwehr Canal.

And so on and violently on. As Hecht scrambled to cover the brutal and often bewildering events that unfolded during this chaotic period, he was getting an education, not just in the complicated ins and outs of postwar German politics or on how to survive on "lousy ersatz nourishment" obtained at "sandbagging prices" along with bouts of scurvy. It was also a crash course in human depravity. His Berlin stint left him, he later wrote, "with a permanent cynicism toward history." Though he would admit that at the time he'd seen the assassinations and battles, the plots and revolts as farce of a most ghoulish sort. It was "as if I had blundered into a side-street Grand Guignol."

And he recounted it all with his usual amused panache, using the tricks he'd learned on the Chicago streets and in the local room. His punchy, beat-reporter attitude was appreciated by many, including an old *Daily News* friend, Harry Hansen, his predecessor at the Berlin bureau. "You are the life of the party," Hansen wrote Hecht. "After ten thousand lugubrious words from all ends of the earth one cable from you will make everybody sit up and smile and feel that there's something after all in getting out a newspaper." Early on in his stay, though, one of his editors, C. H. Dennis, warned Hecht a bit sternly about "surface effects" in his stories. "I am wholly at a loss," Dennis wrote of an interview that Hecht had conducted with Philipp Scheidemann, premier of the new Socialist German Republic, "to understand why you should call [him] an 'affable combination of

Bismarck and Hinky Dink.'" (Hinky Dink was the nickname of a corrupt Chicago alderman of the period.) It was the first interview Scheidemann had granted since the war, and Hecht's approach was, Dennis thought, like "playing leapfrog in the presence of a corpse or whistling in church. I feel that having a great opportunity to get a notable dispatch you first laid out a fine framework, then threw a gob of color on the canvas and went away. The business of interpreting these people is a big, serious business. The world is interested. It is a prodigious opportunity."

So it was, and while Hecht would snap to and get a good deal bigger and more serious in his reporting, in his off hours he continued to school himself in the darkly high spirits and rank absurdity, even perversity, of the historical moment, gallivanting with Grosz and Doehmann around Berlin's nightclubs and to "macabre parties where Lesbians beat up college boys and bemedaled colonels sat with painted children in their laps."

Or he'd attend evenings like the raucous Dada gala held in May of that year, over which Grosz presided and in which "twelve of the most distinguished poets of the Fatherland and one hotel porter" recited their verse simultaneously. Later, according to one of Hecht's predictably mutating descriptions, a race took place between a sewing machine and a typewriter—or maybe it was six typewriters and six sewing machines, accompanied by a swearing contest? No matter. Dada was, he declared, "a cult of laughter," designed to "wipe out every trace of Germanism from Germany—its dripping poetry, its wattled professorialism, its sarcophagi canvases, its musical opium, its Prussian strut, its obsession with greatness." Even though he'd seen firsthand the blood in the streets, the bodies in the prison yard, this "art movement based on a turned stomach and a yell of derision" was, he thought, "the only German revolution."

Throughout his career, Hecht claimed to have spent a full year in Berlin, from the end of 1918 until the start of 1920, though

With Grosz and Doehmann, Berlin

the dates on his news dispatches and a passenger list of the SS *Nieuw Amsterdam* make clear that he and Marie boarded that New York–bound ship in Rotterdam on July 26, 1919, having spent a little more than six months in Europe.

Why he would deliberately fudge this timeline isn't clear, though he could be forgiven if the exact chronology had grown hazy in his memory. It was a dizzy period, and days and weeks, whole years, may well have swirled together. In his 1954 memoir he would briefly describe his return from Germany to the sloped floors and dusty windows of the *Daily News* offices and then announce in a single gulped breath: "During the three years that followed, I wrote a column for the *News* called '1,001 Afternoons in Chicago.' I wrote five books, many short stories and two plays. I published a newspaper of my own called *The Chicago Literary Times*, to which I was the chief and sometimes sole contributor. I went into a high-finance publicity enterprise on the side. Also I fell in love, left my wife and daughter, my grand piano, cloisonné floor lamps, Lillehan rugs and three thousand books, to go away with 'the other woman.'" These were, he proclaimed, among the "most favorite years of my life."

Of course, the saga wasn't nearly as tidy or linear as all that. An endearment-filled letter sent to Marie, out of town soon after their return from Berlin ("how in God's name I'll ever be able to snap back into some sort of an American focus on what constitutes a day's job in this country is more than I can see now . . . I yearn for you"), must have been written just as he was getting to know a soulful twenty-one-year-old recently hired by the *Daily News*, Rose Caylor, that other woman. Carl Sandburg later wrote Hecht of his memories of Rose's "girlish brightness in the local room when she first came within your vision" and recalled being the secret go-between for their letters, which the poet stashed in his desk. Though rumors circulated at the paper that Hecht and Rose were involved, she, for her typically prickly part, remembered that when this bit of gossip began making the rounds, they had engaged in a single "brief, unpleasant conversation" about a book she happened to be carrying—*The Ego and Its Own*, by the German philosopher Max Stirner.

But it was only a matter of time before they did launch a passionate affair—both sexual and verbal—which would not only become the subject of Hecht's soon-to-be-acclaimed first novel, *Erik Dorn*, it would evolve into a close and complicated marriage that would last the rest of their lives. Hecht considered Rose the most emotional woman he'd ever met, and her depth of feeling drew him to her in a kind of stunned wonder.

Rose was also—this mattered to Hecht—Jewish, and her particular strain of Jewishness was as unfamiliar to him as it was fascinating. Intellectual and intense, she had been born in Vilna to a moderately religious father and a University of Warsaw–trained obstetrician mother, a Marxist, who brought her to the United States at age nine. Allegedly able to recite from memory whole chapters of *Das Kapital* by the time she immigrated, Rose learned English by reading the complete works of Dickens, and enrolled as a sixteen-year-old at the University of Chicago, where she was a middling student, excelling in German and "Vocal Interpretation of Poetry," as she struggled with other classes, including Shakespeare's Comedies, Political Economics, and English Composition. But she kept busy at school, writing and performing in one-act plays, participating actively on the debate team (negative rebuttals were a forte), and winning a prize for excellence in oratory. She graduated with a Ph.B. in literature at the ripe old age of twenty. Now she acted with a traveling company, planned to write fiction, and had what another of Hecht's friends and collaborators, Denver-born reporter and later playwright and screenwriter Gene Fowler, called a "fighting heart." She seemed to him "a sort of ageless sprite, and ready to take on the champions of all branches of combat either single-handed or en masse." Having fallen in love with the *News*'s star reporter, Rose would devote herself to

Rose Caylor

him utterly. From the start of their romance and to death, in fact, she remained almost violently committed to the cause of Ben Hecht and his brilliance. He was not nearly so monomaniacal, or monogamous, in his adoration, but he did love her seriously, and in ways both broad and basic, Rose would play a critical role in shaping the man that he was becoming.

The start of their clandestine affair and the composition of *Erik Dorn* were simultaneous, and as both gestated, they informed each other. The book concerns a newsman who both is and isn't a stand-in for Hecht. An editor at a Chicago paper, Dorn doesn't aspire to be an artist, and he's more middle-aged than Hecht was at the time, though the title character shares the young novelist's mordant outlook, as well as his acrobatic verbal gifts. Dorn feels himself essentially empty, and his facility with words creates a wall between himself and the world: "Carried away in the heat of some intricate debate he would pause internally, as his voice continued without interruption, and exclaim to himself, 'What in hell am I talking about?' And a momentary awe would overcome him—the awe of listening to himself give utterance to fantastic ideas that he knew had no existence in him—a cynical magician watching a white rabbit he had never seen before crawl naively out of his own sleeve." At the start of the novel, he's married to the pliant and uncomplicated Anna and respected by his colleagues, who view him as "a normal-seeming, kindly individual who wore his linen and his features with a certain politely exotic air—the air of an identity."

All of that changes when he's jolted into powerful emotion by the appearance of a young, Russian-born Jewish artist named Rachel Laskin—"a morose little girl insanely sensitive and with a dream inside her"—and his whole sturdy if sneering sense of reality begins to crumble. Much melodrama ensues as he leaves Anna for Rachel, Rachel leaves him, he veers in and out of hallucination, despair, ecstasy and then is shipped off to Berlin, where he finds himself amid the postwar German chaos, filing newspaper stories about Spartacists and socialists, Scheidemann and Liebknecht. Returning to America, he desperately seeks out both Anna and Rachel, and both reject him. He shuffles back to the local room and the emptiness with which he started.

Though he would dedicate the novel to Marie ("guiltily," Rose claimed) and had apparently begun writing it before he met Rose, when he had been conducting an unconsummated flirtation with a reporter named Esther Cohen, there seems to have been no doubt in his mind as the pages piled up about his true muse: "Rachel is changing despite me," he wrote Rose. "She was Esther . . . Now she is you . . . she is entirely you . . . I write with your gestures and voice in my head . . . With the feel of you in my fingers . . . You wrap yourself around every breath of me and I can't get away from you . . . When I rewrite I'll stick in the little phrases, hints of background quick strokes hither and yon to distract the reader from the reality of Erik and Rachel. What hits you wrong is that they're real . . . You expect, as does everybody who reads, I included—the pleasantly worked out subterfuges, the slick stage managing which takes the place of reality and gives you paper mache." He feared, he wrote, "sacrilege" in attempting to capture her in words. "If I can get Rachel down one tenth as beautifully as I know you, I'll have done Something."

Boosted by an aggressive advertising campaign by his publisher, Putnam, announcing the arrival of "the biggest luminary in the literary firmament," the book appeared in September 1921, and the response was immediate and fierce, both for and against. "Here is a novel that glares, dazzles, startles with its clear shine," proclaimed the critic of the *Brooklyn Eagle*. "If you want to hear the most powerful voice of the present generation . . . read . . . this first novel by a writer who is destined to make a tremendous place for himself." The *Hartford Courant* was far less impressed, dismissing it as "a futile book . . . a complete and most pretentious failure . . . from any sane and sensible view point, beneath contempt."

Mencken also weighed in, offering a more nuanced account in *The Smart Set*, where he called the novel "a curious piece of work indeed—half tale and half rhapsody. . . . Superficially, it seems to be the story of a young husband's gradual revolt against domestic normalcy; actually it is the chronicle of a sensitive soul's anomalistic reactions to the whole phantasmagoria of modern civilization—the spiritual knee-jerks of a genuine original. The thing, in spots, is almost unintelligible; the author gropes, but his own ideas seem to elude him. But in other spots it reaches an amazing clarity and brilliancy."

Francis Hackett, writing in the *New Republic*, offered a respectful but still more critical assessment, admiring the "dynamic energy" of the story while noting that "a style like Mr. Hecht's [is] sure to be lavishly praised. . . . For myself, I find its novelty as tiresome as too many fuchsia gowns. . . . It is, I believe, an actual straining for impressiveness, for accent, for effect."

The fuchsia-gown effect is hard to deny. Although lacking almost any trace of Hecht's sharp sense of humor—perhaps he'd taken critics like Pound too much at their word when they urged him to stop goofing around—the book contains at least a dash of almost every other possible seasoning he could grab off the literary spice rack. Writing in terms now florid, now cerebral, now realistic, expressionistic, bodice-ripping, symbolic, and brokenly associative, Hecht seemed intent on packing between two covers all the prose forms he'd ever encountered, each of the emotions he'd ever experienced, along with every perception he'd ever registered—of Chicago's streets, Berlin's bars, sex, journalism, marriage, war, Middle America, political radicalism, and the putative spiritual nothingness of modern life. It was audacious. It was exhausting. As another ur-Chicago writer, Nelson Algren, put it decades later, no American had "written a novel this good yet this bad."

Not long after the Hechts returned home from Berlin (as Ben was sneaking out for trysts with Rose and writing *Erik Dorn*), they found themselves again in debt. Marie had insisted on buying a four-story house that looked to Hecht like "an impressive summer hotel." A new car, three servants, and regular, lavish entertaining added to their expenses, and in order to pay off their bills, he left his job at the paper and became a partner in a public relations firm. The endeavor proved extremely lucrative—hype came naturally to Hecht—but the work made him miserable.

And so it was that one rainy day in the spring of 1921 he marched back into the *Daily News* building and straight to the desk of his former editor Henry Justin Smith, who later described what ensued with a flair that sounds downright Hechtian: "He had," wrote Smith, "been divorced from our staff for some weeks, and had married an overdressed, blatant creature called Publicity." The alliance was, declared Hecht, unhappy. And now here he was with a new idea for the paper—"Something different. Maybe impossible."

What Hecht proposed to Smith that day was the column that would become "A Thousand and One Afternoons in Chicago"—an undertaking at once journalistic and literary, small in form and large in implication, casual on its surface and profound at its heart. The idea, as he outlined it for his once and future editor, was "that just under the edge of the news as commonly understood, the news often flatly and unimaginatively told, lay life; that in this urban life there dwelt the stuff of literature, not hidden in remote places, either, but walking the downtown streets, peering from the windows of sky scrapers, sunning itself in parks and boulevards." Hecht saw himself as "its interpreter." He wanted, wrote Smith, to be "the lens throwing city life into new colors . . . the microscope revealing its contortions in life and death."

Smith wisely agreed on the spot, and the pieces that Hecht began to write and Smith to publish daily, starting in June of that year and continuing until October 1922, reveal a side, or sides, of Hecht that he hadn't managed to express in his more grandiose and belabored attempts at high art. Dashed off in a zigzagging range of modes that all somehow seem of a generous and cohesive whole, the stories were, as Smith put it, "seemingly born out of nothing," and appeared on the paper's back page, alongside the comic strips. The heroes of these decidedly antiheroic bits and pieces are Poles and blacks, Swedes and Jews, and everyone in between. They are a beleaguered mother of nine, Mrs. Sardotopolis, and "the venerable and somewhat Gargantuan" Gustave, who cares for nothing in the world besides fixing watches at a shop on North Wells Street. They are Bill Cochran, a tobacco-chewing deputy sheriff who plays cards with men condemned to hang for their crimes within hours, and Peewee, a heavily lipsticked manicurist who explains matter-of-factly how she handles lecherous clients at the barbershop where she works. They are the black vaudevillian Bert Williams, whom Hecht audaciously imagines joining company in the afterlife with "the Great Actors who have died since the day of Euripides . . . [and who] sit around in their favorite makeups in the Valhalla reserved for all good and glorious Thespians." They are the homesick Sing Lee, who writes poems to his beloved Canton after hours at his Lake Park Avenue laundry. They are men fishing dreamily off the Municipal Pier and figures lying quietly in the grass at Grant Park. They are Chicago, and they are, in a peculiar and refreshingly unself-centered way, also all Ben Hecht.

"The newspaper reporter got an idea one day," wrote Hecht, using the handle he'd assigned his own character in these columns, "that the city was nothing more nor less than a vast, broken mirror giving him back garbled images of himself." Unlike Erik Dorn, or Moisse the "young dramatist," though, the newspaper reporter looks *beyond* his own ego and feels part of the human tragicomedy unfolding around him, and this essential sense of identification lends the "Thousand and One Afternoons" a poignancy, expansiveness, and warmth mostly absent from his fiction. Which isn't to say that he avoided fictionalizing here—or melancholy. By naming the column as he had,

Hecht had cast himself as a kind of hard-boiled, Middle American Scheherazade, for whom spinning yarns had become a means of survival.

Words now poured out of him with an almost frightening force and pace. They splashed into his daily columns for the *News* and erupted into a second novel, the blistering, *Babbitt*-like *Gargoyles;* they flowed into a smooth stage comedy, *The Egotist;* they streamed into a whimsical murder mystery, *The Florentine Dagger,* which he claimed he dictated, on a bet, in thirty-six hours. They gushed forth in impassioned geysers of letters to Rose, and hovered in the smoky air at Schlogl's, the old-world tavern near the *Daily News* where, amid the polished spittoons and black walnut tables, he and a regular crowd (Sandburg, Sherwood Anderson, Harry Hansen, Henry Justin Smith, and a rotating cast of literary- and newspapermen) gathered weekly for baby turkey, eel in aspic, "owls to order," and nearly endless conversation, which Hecht tended to dominate. "One might as well try to stop a mill-race," wrote Hansen of Hecht's virtuosic lunchtime talk, "but no one wants to."

This word-flood ran both hot and cold, alternating between an apparently unbounded love of the world and the blackest misanthropy. "Into this book I am putting," he promised in a letter to the critic Burton Rascoe while he was working on *Gargoyles,* "all the venom I have stored against the human race during twenty-eight years of much too intimate contact with it, and much too intimate a knowledge of my own not too blameless soul. I am, in fine, attempting to show the hidden strings which motivate the actions, hypocrisies, primpings and postures of the comically idiotic little vermin who are the salt of the earth and the backbone of our grand and glorious country." He would do nothing short of "condens[e] 'Madame Bovary' into a paragraph and 'The Idiot' into a page."

Hecht had first lobbed this angry book at Putnam, whose

editors found it compelling but suggested cuts. Hecht insisted that the book be printed exactly as written, and when Putnam hesitated, he withdrew the manuscript and sent it to Horace Liveright, home with a head cold in New Rochelle. Then visiting New York, Hecht was leaving by train in six hours. He gave Liveright this deadline to accept—along with the same condition that not a word be changed. The canny publisher of the Modern Library, Freud, Dreiser, Pound, and T. S. Eliot agreed, though according to Hansen, the book that appeared with the firm of Boni and Liveright in the autumn of 1922 was printed "practically in the form suggested by Putnam, with certain offending lines neatly dropped somewhere between New York and New Rochelle."

This book, too, was greeted with emphatic if severely mixed reviews, which Liveright—as much the showman as Hecht—had decided to milk for all their controversial worth, taking out multiple newspaper ads proclaiming that many critics were calling it "the greatest realistic novel of the generation" while others were "reviling it as the most exaggerated, unpleasant and despicable misrepresentation of human motives and reactions of all generations. But"—the clincher—"everybody has something to say about it." The gambit worked. In Boston, the Watch and Ward Society lodged obscenity charges, and *Gargoyles* rocketed up the best-seller list.

These various provocations were really just a prelude, though, to the major scandal that Hecht seemed determined to churn up. In September 1922, the same month that *Gargoyles* appeared, the Chicago booksellers Pascal Covici and William F. McGee—a Rumanian-born Jew and a former priest, whose cluttered Washington Street shop was a popular gathering place for the local literati—issued a limited, mail-order edition of a book by Hecht described in an unsigned prospectus as "without question the most daring psychological melodrama of modern writing." The work in question, *Fantazius Mallare: A Mysterious*

Oath, was actually a revision of a novel he'd written several years earlier and stashed in a drawer, where it probably should have stayed—and probably *would* have, if he hadn't had his heart set on goading John Sumner and his Society for the Suppression of Vice into banning something, anything, from his pen.

Perversity, then, if not actual perversion, was what drove Hecht to offer up this overheated exercise in adolescent self-indulgence. Meant as an homage to decadents like Oscar Wilde and Joris-Karl Huysmans, the book takes shape instead as an often preposterous sexual phantasmagoria about the relations between an insane artist, a gypsy girl, and a black hunchbacked dwarf named Goliath. The book is marked by prose so silly and pseudosalacious it seems plain Hecht was daring the authorities, daring Sumner, to object: "Ah, what loathsome and lecherous mouths women are!" reads one typical passage. "Offering their urine ducts as a mystic Paradise! Stretching themselves on their backs and seducing egoists with the unctuous lie of possession." To ensure maximum readerly outrage he enlisted an artist friend, Wallace Smith, to render a series of pornographically stylized, Aubrey Beardsley–esque ink drawings of bare, erect penises, along with an illustration of a naked man, face down, his pelvis thrust into a busty female tree trunk.

But all of that was really a stunt. The one stab at real literary daring that Hecht took in the book was the opening salvo, a defiant declaration that "this dark and wayward book is affectionately dedicated to my enemies . . . the curious ones who take fanatic pride in disliking me . . . the baffling ones who remain enthusiastically ignorant of my existence . . . the moral ones upon whom Beauty exercises a lascivious and corrupting influence . . ." and so on, with a kind of cackling gusto, for a high-flying, nonstop, eight-page-long tour de force of a sentence that's said to have inspired Allen Ginsberg's "Howl" and that is the book's sole redeeming feature.

It may also have been the nose-thumbing flourish that finally got him what he wanted—into trouble with the law. This took some doing. The copies Covici sent out to critics garnered little response; neither did the fifty displayed in the store window, opened to especially risqué passages. Finally, the postal authorities obliged Hecht's desperate yearning for attention by warning Covici to stop selling the book. When he ignored them, federal warrants were issued, charging Hecht, Smith, and the publishers with "conspiracy to circulate obscene matter by means of interstate common carriers." They scrounged together bail, and though it took several years for the trial to play itself out, with Clarence Darrow serving as defense attorney, and both Mencken and Liveright offering themselves as character witnesses for Hecht, the "conspirators" eventually pleaded *nolo contendere*. The episode ended with more of a whimper than the bang Hecht had fantasized: he was fined $1,000 and lost his job at the *Daily News*.

Max Bodenheim had decamped from Chicago for Greenwich Village some time before, but in late 1922 Hecht heard he was back, and sent up a friendly flare. "After seven years," he wrote, "you and I are still the best hated men in American literature. Why not pool our persecution mania? My hate is getting monotonous. I confess that even yours lacks variety. I will be here Monday at 4 with a bottle of gin. I shall expect you. I salute the possibility of your fatheadedness." Soon the men were working together on the project that would prove the last hurrah of this stage of their lives, what one commentator has called "a parody of the serious days of the Renaissance," the satirical tabloid known as the *Chicago Literary Times*.

The policy of the paper was, according to its editor, Hecht, "to attack everything," though it seemed less an earnest assault than it did one of those furious German Dada demonstrations translated into a tap-dancing American street corner act. If anything, there was a carnival aspect to the enterprise: Hecht planned to launch the first issue with a parade featuring brass bands, a calliope, and half a mile of floats, all bearing Chicago writers hard at work. (Unfortunately, this never happened.) He resurrected his "Afternoons" column for the *Times*, while he and Bodenheim wrote much of the rest of the paper under various pseudonyms—Hubert Handshake, Oscar Vraiment—and joined forces on a serialized send-up of censors and censorship, "Cutie, A Warm Mama." They published a list of the world's twenty-two worst books and a comical diatribe about New York literary magazines, "continually talking about Art as if it were their dead grandmother." A pan of eleven new volumes of poetry appeared under the headline "BODENHEIM RUNS AMUCK: SIX KILLED; FIVE INJURED." Wallace Smith and George Grosz contributed regular drawings, Covici served as "manager" (publisher), and, signing with just their initials, Marie and Rose wrote occasional articles—often squaring off in print, with scathing, barely veiled assaults on each other's characters.

Although the Hechts' marriage was already in trouble, the women's proximity on those pages probably speeded its end. Marie had known about the affair for some time, and though Ben didn't deny it, he refused either to leave his wife or stop seeing his mistress, and at a certain point even proposed splitting his nights between them. The female players in this drama were, not unreasonably, miserable with the arrangement, but he seemed smugly willing to keep it in place and was unapologetic about his position: "If I have to choose between you and Marie," he wrote Rose, "I will choose you. But I'm not ready to get rid of a mode of life into which I have grown."

However different in background and bearing, Marie and Rose were both gifted, highly verbal women, and each would eventually exact narrative revenge with her own book-length account of these painful events. Marie's memoir appeared anonymously in 1932 as *My First Husband,* by His First Wife, though all in the know knew just who was who: "Eric Mayer," the title character, was the brilliant young author of works including the column "A Million Mornings in Chicago" and a scandalous book called *A Malarial Fantasy.* Rose's volley was a transparently autobiographical 1927 novel, *The Woman on the Balcony.* In Marie's version, Rose is painted as something of a stalker and a hysteric: "She was what I would call a furniture actress; of the throwiest type," Marie writes, describing Rose's performance in a play. "She would come on the stage, fix a bureau with her eyes and plunge toward it, bringing up with her arms draped over its top. That would not satisfy her long. She would swim with her arms toward a chair and melt into its depth. A moment later her emotions would drive her relentlessly toward another piece of furniture." Despite her desire to mock Rose and punish Hecht publicly, Marie proved herself a fine comic writer with this book, as if to show that whatever else they had taken from her, she'd held fast to her sense of humor: "I had thought I was a genius for a while—until I married one who simply reeked with laurel," she explains at the outset. "Then I discovered that it takes a genius of a certain kind to live with a genius." Her chronicle of their marriage is, understandably, a searing indictment of his character, though what's more surprising is that a certain lingering tenderness also creeps in: "When I married him I sacrificed . . . many of my ambitions. Eric was indeed a career. You could no more escape his strident bids for attention than you could live in the same house with an anaconda and ignore it. When not transfixed by his oriental fascination, one was smothered in the coils of his excitements, a crushing process all the more deadly; for in his intellectual woods there was always a tree around which he could coil his tail. Yet Eric at times was a child, a three-ring circus and a wailing-wall all in one—and I loved him."

In Rose's book, meanwhile, and for obvious reasons—she

and Hecht were married by the time she published it—he's conjured mostly in adoring and even reverential terms. ("There is
no way . . . to describe him in this most intimate phase of his
life, without mentioning the man he was to be—a man of au-
thoritative genius . . .") Her vehement devotion notwithstanding, Rose was also capable of stepping back and describing her
lover with a knowing, even Jamesian, detachment: "As he talked,"
she writes, "his smile became far away from her, cold, seemingly; his face, to her, had almost an unfamiliar appearance, a
look of secret energy was on it, an aloof mental existence (people always felt they were interrupting him when they addressed
him, because of this air of energy, this separate existence which
he maintained among them). . . . He talked like a boy and like
a savant, perhaps the ridiculous savant whom one reads about
so often in the newspapers, who talks Greek to his child in the
hope that it will absorb knowledge in the same way that children absorb the usual nonsense . . ."

Not surprisingly, however, Rose aims her sharpest darts at
"Margaret," i.e., Marie, "a sordid enemy" with "blond eyes"
and an "obvious, Anglo-Saxon face." According to Rose, Margaret struck her husband as "merely coarse. . . . She seemed to
have undergone a startling change in the direction of medioc-
rity, all her stupidities had come startlingly into view." In both
books, as apparently in real life, the women met at a restaurant
to discuss their triangular conundrum, and in Rose's version,
sitting there, she decided of Margaret/Marie that "she hated her
hat. And later, when Margaret walked away from her, she noticed and hated her shoes. . . . Whether she was too fat or too
broad, or because her hair was soiled, or because she wore a
large diamond ornament on a thin chain around her large neck,
she was infinitely less than the idea of her."

Reading these sniping accounts back to back is sometimes
entertaining but more often sad. In general, one feels trapped
in an especially claustrophobic hall of mirrors—where, as Marie

put it in her own book, "their typewriters worked overtime at the slightest provocation."

Hecht did eventually make the break and moved into a rooming house just north of downtown with Rose. Their quarters were tight, and though they seemed happy, he had entered into a kind of holding pattern as he wrote yet another autobiographical novel, *Humpty Dumpty*, concocted a feeble sequel to *Mallare*, and played his violin. Rose scribbled and typed. They waited for Marie to grant him a divorce so that they could marry.

But Hecht was waiting in more sense than one. Given all his accomplishments, it seemed, in fact, that he was still waiting to decide just what he wanted to *be* when he grew up. At around this time, Harry Hansen closed his book about this period and place and its literary people, *Midwest Portraits*, with an essay on Hecht, calling him "the most baffling, and for that reason the most promising writer of the whole Chicago group. . . . With Ben Hecht anything is possible. . . . He is to-day a man whose promise is better than his performance, whose gifts are better than he knows, whose mental processes cry aloud for discipline and direction. . . . To-morrow may find him a prophet and a seer; to-day he stands there, a Pagliacci on the fire escape, singing his heart out over the streets and alleys of a city whose very stones he loves but whose people fill him with sad and mournful soliloquies."

By now, though, the love of those stones had started to fade. In his last "Afternoons" column, published in the *Literary Times* in June of 1924, Hecht admitted, "It would be much more intelligent to put an end to this game of pretending the city panorama fascinates me as it once did." His friends threw him a final blowout lunch at Schlogl's; then he and Rose packed their bags and prepared to go.

The lights of the town would dim a few watts without him. "In a way," muses one literary historian, "Chicago of the twen-

Last lunch at Schlogl's

ties was the Age of Hecht," while another old newspaper friend would write in his memoirs that Hecht gave the Chicago Renaissance "so much color and sensation that there are times when I see him as pretty much the whole movement."

This wasn't just backward-looking overstatement. On the summer day when Rose and Hecht made their way to the LaSalle Street train station, a notice appeared on the front page of one of the *Daily News*'s rival papers:

"FLAGS AT HALFMAST. BEN HECHT IS LEAVING CHICAGO."

4

The Times

By 1924, the party had picked up and moved to New York—
"a phony, smart-aleck, fat-headed town," in the words of
Hecht's closest collaborator-to-be, Charles MacArthur, who'd
also recently hopped a train east, fleeing a failed first marriage
and in search of fresh stimulation. Like Hecht, MacArthur
had worked the city beat in Chicago, but now he declared himself done with journalism, having arrived in Manhattan, which
was, he announced, "for press agents, not newspapermen. . . .
You've got to love a town to be a reporter in it . . . and, baby, I
don't love."

Hecht described things a bit differently and later mused
that throughout their lives he and MacArthur "remained newspaper reporters and continued to keep our hats on before the
boss, drop ashes on the floor and disdain all practical people."
Working for rival papers, they had been friends in Chicago but
grew much closer after both landed in New York and bonded

over their nostalgia for the "stockyard Athens" they'd left behind on the shores of Lake Michigan. Now, though, since MacArthur was "hotly in love with the theater" and Hecht announced himself "ready to work on anything," they threw themselves into their collective next act by writing for the stage as a team.

Hecht mentions work. In fact, a great deal of play propelled this endeavor, since the categories often fused when Ben and Charlie conspired. It wasn't just that in the course of a typical writing session—as Hecht sat with pencil, paper, and his trusty lapboard, and the endlessly distractable MacArthur paced, lay on the couch, doodled, stared out the window—they took frequent breaks for Parcheesi, cards, backgammon. The process of batting back and forth zippy dialogue and narrative twists *itself* became a game of the most fruitful sort. They took their playing seriously, in other words, and put it to good use. And this was perhaps the key to their long-term partnership in crime and creativity: Hecht and MacArthur were each sharpest when they were horsing around intently and even rigorously—together.

"The boys" (so they were widely known) may have romped in their own private way—they liked to refer euphemistically to their "lively doings"—but the whole of New York had in these years been seized by a strong urge to rollick. Every cliché of hedonistic Jazz Age America seems to have been on frothy tap in that time and place. An apparently oceanic supply of bootleg booze fueled weeklong benders, wild parties, frantic extramarital coupling. So much so that the line between getting dropdown drunk and getting down to literary business could often blur dangerously. By the time Hecht came to town, the dashing, lady-killing, chronically hungover MacArthur and his no less dashing, lady-killing, hungover pal, satirist and theater critic Robert Benchley, with whom he lived on Madison Avenue, were fixtures at the Algonquin Round Table, where much of their verbal brilliance was famously written on air. "Self-expression,

Charles MacArthur

as literature is called," according to Hecht, "seemed extraneous toil for these roommates, who felt themselves fully expressed when they put on their shoes at noon."

The son of a fire-and-brimstone-preaching evangelist father who regularly lashed his children's bare backs with a vinegar-soaked strap, MacArthur appeared to be making up for lost time as a sinner—an impulse eased in this new setting by the fact that, as Hecht put it, "the town MacArthur didn't like fell in love with him." During his early days in New York, before Hecht's arrival, he seemed poised, in fact, to become the victim of his own puckish sex appeal, which made him the darling of the city's smart set as it also often kept him from the less glamorous act of sitting still and setting words to paper. Another Algonquin-frequenting drama critic, the portly tastemaker Alexander Woollcott, claimed credit for discovering MacArthur, and showed him off to the so-called Vicious Circle like some exotic pet. It was in that quippy, caustic context that MacArthur met Dorothy Parker, who fell hard for him. And the rest is gossip-column history, as he broke her heart and got her pregnant, allegedly chipping in thirty dollars for an abortion before loping off to his next conquest. "It serves me right," she brooded sharply, "for putting all my eggs in one bastard."

During these years, a bash seemed always to be erupting somewhere. Or maybe it was all one long bash. And while the guest list to this never-ending shindig remained fairly constant and star-studded, the location shifted around. One night, the festivities would spring up at the Hell's Kitchen apartment Woollcott shared with his war buddy Harold Ross, a high school dropout from Colorado then struggling to launch a magazine his friends were skeptical about, and which he wanted to call *The New Yorker.* Another night, they'd swing into action at the West 48th Street brownstone where publishing playboy Horace Liveright housed both his editorial and theatrical production offices in high if eccentric style.

Several of Hecht's best friends were the life of this constant party. Besides MacArthur, Herman Mankiewicz became one of Hecht's closest companions during these years. Another deeply gifted, heavy-drinking wit and former reporter who dabbled at playwriting, he held jobs as second-string theater reviewer at the *New York Times* and as the first-ever drama critic for Ross's new magazine. Meanwhile, "Mank," or "Manky," as Hecht called him, seems to have spilled much of his best material into the ears of his tipsy friends instead of onto the page. Hecht described his "thrown-away genius, his modesty, his shrug at adversity," as well as his swiftness of thought and the ferocity of his insight. "He could puncture egos, draw blood from pretenses—and his victims, with souls abashed, still sat and laughed."

Hardly a teetotaler or wallflower, Hecht was pleased to find himself "in some demand at week ends full of ping pong and headliners," but preferred to remain at a wary remove from the more extreme forms of carousing and catty chatter then in vogue. And while he was casually friendly with many of its members, the Algonquin "school of wags" in particular struck him as a menace to any aspiring writer's development. "The artist was wise who was absent," he'd assert. "For a young novelist or playwright with his roots not yet down, to sit in such a clique of know-it-alls was to get the art frightened out of him. A pickpocket keeping company with a pack of boastful cops might feel similarly hesitant toward the practice of his profession." Despite his good-time garrulousness, a certain detachment, combined with an allergy to any form of consensus and a fairly compulsive addiction to work—arguably, Hecht's own drug of choice—kept him out of at least this sort of trouble.

MacArthur had no such powers of self-preservation, though once he met and fell in love with the actress and Sunday mass–attending good girl Helen Hayes in 1924, he did start trying harder to focus. And Hecht played a major role in getting MacArthur to concentrate, as MacArthur offered the prematurely jaded Hecht a necessary jolt of enthusiasm: "I needed," Hecht would admit, "somebody else's love of the stage as a stimulant." That his own passion for the theater was considerably milder than Charlie's he confessed, claiming he was "never a true playwright." The medium didn't lure him urgently, as writing novels did. More than that, he had to "overcome an aversion" before setting foot in a theater, where he felt "out of place . . . as if I had intruded on an alien house of worship."

Given Hecht's distaste and MacArthur's almost pathological lack of discipline, it's remarkable that within a short time the pair were able to dream up a major hit, nothing less than the 1928 play—*The Front Page*, their ode to the rowdy Chicago newspaper world of their youth—that Tennessee Williams later declared made it possible for him to conceive his own work. "They paved the way for me," he told Helen Hayes. "They took the corsets off American theater." In the seventies British critic Kenneth Tynan described it as "the best American comedy ever written." And some twenty years on, playwright Tom Stoppard pronounced it "the 'only' American comedy of the 1920s in the way that '[The] Importance [of Being Earnest]' is the 'only' English comedy of the 1890s. . . . I don't know any play which sustains its verve so well."

But that acclaim came later (as did another hit, *Twentieth Century*, which the *New York Times* called "outrageous, impudent and funny" when it opened in late 1932). The play Hecht himself considered their best was neither of these, but their first, *The Moonshooter*, which materialized almost out of thin air, in the course of the boisterous summer of 1925, spent in a cottage near Woodstock. They hadn't retreated to the countryside with plans to collaborate. When Hecht wasn't cranking out short stories to pay the bills and MacArthur tooting on his harmonica, they tossed horseshoes and lolled by the swimming hole. Helen was away on tour, but Rose was there with them, writing her first novel, frying steaks, and baking blueberry muffins for the many guests who turned up, all with empty pockets and enormous appetites. Harpo, Groucho, Chico, and Zeppo Marx surfaced with a whole cavalcade of wives, girlfriends, children. Rose's lively younger sister, Minna, a psychiatrist in training, appeared, as did Mankiewicz, toting a pair of suitcases filled

With Rose

with nothing but sixteen bottles of Scotch, which he spent two weeks nursing quietly on the couch before his wife, Sara (or "Poor Sara," as she was generally known), arrived to escort him back to Manhattan.

And on rainy days, to pass the time, Ben and Charlie joined forces and wrote. The "loud and comic" play that emerged over several drizzly weeks centers on a man named Enoch, who rescues a female murderer from death row, trundles her off to

Honduras, where he blunders into a war involving a coffee warehouse, the British navy, and a California sheriff. When they finished writing, they traveled to the Long Island home of half-deaf Broadway producer Sam Harris, to whom they read all three acts at the top of their lungs. He thought it very funny and promised to produce it—provided they rewrite the ending, in which Enoch was shot dead. "You can't kill a hero like that in a comedy," Harris insisted, though before they had time to consider revisions, they returned to the city, bumped into Mankiewicz, set out for a night on the town, and (so Hecht's the-cat-ate-my-homework account has it) promptly misplaced their only two copies of the script.

While they lost *The Moonshooter*, they had—by writing it—found a recipe for working together. Some alchemical combination of Hecht's ribald wit, his lucidity, brashness, and drive and MacArthur's ribald wit, his exactitude, reserve, and charm made them perfect complements. Though MacArthur never managed to write much on his own—he had trouble finishing anything, was modest to a fault, and seemed often to find himself hovering in a partner's shadow, whether Hecht's or Helen Hayes's—he played a major if hard-to-quantify role in the composition of some of Hecht's finest writing for both stage and screen. He also seemed to have brought out an unusual kind of selflessness and calm in his best friend. The almost-always combative Hecht would later claim that in all their years of collaborating there was "never any debate between us," and would ascribe to MacArthur "quicker perception than anyone I have ever known," as he conjured his friend's "tang [and] sweetness." He called MacArthur "more than a man of great talent . . . himself a great piece of writing." But Hecht was an excellent piece of writing, too. And for years afterward—in New York, in Hollywood, in the Hudson River–side town of Nyack, where Charlie had been raised and where, over a picnic lunch one summer afternoon soon after they started working together, "the boys" and Helen and Rose resolved to settle down one day for good—the ingredients would remain the same: Ben and Charlie, the lapboard and pencil, the pacing and doodling, the play.

Despite Hecht's resistance to the various forms of celebrity worship and social climbing surrounding him in New York, he was fascinated by the city where he happened upon not only a trusted writing partner and Broadway success, but also its "greatest oddity . . . its Jews."

Until he had landed in Manhattan, Hecht said, he'd considered himself "un-Jewish," a state that he'd entered without any particular effort or self-awareness. Living in Racine and Chicago, he'd felt himself "a Jew by accident" and considered his Jewishness something he'd been able to shed as easily as one would rid oneself of a childhood nickname.

In New York, however, the sheer number of Jews he encountered made him far more self-conscious, and curious. Within a month of arriving, he'd met more Jews than he'd ever known. And they were, as he marveled later, "without accent, and not remotely connected to tailoring—a novelty to me who had known only the Jewish voices and needle-ish activities of my family." Still more astonishing, they dominated the city's culture. Although Hecht was proud of the ubiquity and accomplishment of these New York Jews—who, he noted, ran many of its theaters and publishing houses, wrote its songs, plays, poetry, and a good swath of its newspaper columns, gave its concerts, threw its swankiest parties, owned its department stores—he was also perplexed by what he viewed as a desire on the part of many of these ubiquitous and accomplished Jews to deliberately squelch their Semitism. He viewed this as a pretense that "lies in the delusion that, having ceased to be a Jew, you have become something else." While for Hecht "un-Jewishness" had been an unconscious product of circumstance, these New York Jews were, he believed, straining, even *aspiring*, to suppress their backgrounds "out of fear, rather than out of sacrilege or indifference." Ironically, this fear "kept them as vulnerably Jewish as if they attended their First Nights and Croquet Tournaments with talliths around their shoulders."

It's probably worth taking Hecht's disquisitions on this complex subject with a grain of kosher salt (by the time he wrote these words, he'd had his Jewish consciousness raised through the roof by the Holocaust), but he also seems to have been genuinely swept up in a real-time romance with this cultural context and all it implied for his ever-evolving sense of self. "Perversely," he would write, "in this center of un-Judaizing, I began to turn into a Jew."

Soon after that summer in Woodstock, at what he called in retrospect "the peak of all my shaygetz [non-Jewish] activities"—and, oddly, right around the time he contrived to earn some quick money by dashing off a silly but stinging satirical novel called *Count Bruga,* based on a caricature of his very first real Jewish friend, Max Bodenheim, recast as the drunken and lecherous poet Jules Ganz, who goes abroad and returns to New York, having reimagined himself as a nobleman with a red beard and a high silk hat—he and Rose found themselves in a Manhattan taxi with MacArthur, looking for an apartment that they might share. As they cruised southward, Charlie became uneasy, announcing at 23rd Street that "a foot further in this direction meant exile." He got out, wished them luck, and "headed back nervously for civilization."

Hecht and Rose proceeded downtown, and as the neighborhoods turned shabbier, he grew more entranced. As he later recounted: "I looked out of the cab window and saw sidewalks crawling with infants, push carts hung with ties, alarm clocks and bananas, old gentlemen in linen frock coats smoothing their whiskers, mothers screaming out of windows, little boys and girls playing hide-and-go-seek in refuse barrels"—and, eventually, a sign announcing an apartment for rent. And so it was that this couple of lapsed, literary Jews found themselves living on Henry Street, at the heart of the very Lower East Side ghetto where Hecht's own life began.

They lasted there for seven months, till the smell of rotting rat corpses in the walls drove them scrambling back uptown, to sweeter-smelling quarters and other concerns. While Hecht's "Jewish non-Jewish friends" considered this interlude "a burst of eccentricity," he insisted it hadn't been. Rather, "I loved something faraway and had spent a while looking at its ghost."

5

The Screen

THE MOST LEGENDARY TELEGRAM in American movie history reached Ben Hecht sometime late in 1926 as he lay in bed, depressed, in the top-floor Beekman Place apartment to which he and Rose had ascended after their brief ghetto stint. Finally married, they were two months behind on their rent, Hecht owed Marie alimony, and, at a loss about where the next cash infusion would come from, he'd sought historical perspective (or maybe dramatic diversion) by crawling under the covers to read *The Decline and Fall of the Roman Empire*. Toward the middle of volume twelve, the doorbell rang. It was Herman Mankiewicz, by way of Western Union, writing from what Hecht would later describe as "the unknown Scythian wastes of Hollywood, Calif.":

WILL YOU ACCEPT THREE HUNDRED PER WEEK TO WORK FOR
PARAMOUNT PICTURES. ALL EXPENSES PAID. THE THREE HUN-
DRED IS PEANUTS. MILLIONS ARE TO BE GRABBED OUT HERE

AND YOUR ONLY COMPETITION IS IDIOTS. DON'T LET THIS GET
AROUND.

The deal was for real—Mankiewicz had apparently stormed
the office of his boss at the studio, B. P. Schulberg, and demanded he hire Hecht, offering to tear up his own contract if
his pal failed to write a hit—but that last secretive aside was just
Manky being sly: the very idea, of course, was for "this" to "get
around," and quickly. Mankiewicz was, as Pauline Kael put
it, "a man who lived to talk, a man who saw moviemaking as
too crazy, too profitable, and too *easy* not to share with one's
friends." Among the first of the New York literati of this period
to set his sights on Hollywood and its pleasantly plump paychecks, Mankiewicz had made his way to the West Coast earlier that year. Soon after sending that cable to Hecht, he'd been
armed with what became known unofficially as the Herman J.
Mankiewicz Fresh Air Fund, charged by Schulberg with recruit-
ing New York playwrights, novelists, newspapermen, and any
and all Algonquin wits to cook up crackling dialogue on a deadline. The screen was then still mute, and although writers had
previously been considered a waste of money, sound was due in
town any minute now, and once the microphones were switched
on, a new attitude toward words would become necessary.

The full-scale invasion of Hollywood by what gossip columnist Louella Parsons dismissively dubbed "eastern scribblers"—
including F. Scott Fitzgerald, Dorothy Parker, George S. Kaufman, Lillian Hellman, Maxwell Anderson, Nunnally Johnson,
Ring Lardner, Moss Hart, Nathanael West, and his brother-in-
law, S. J. Perelman, among many talented others—would come
a bit later. For now, Mankiewicz was a pioneer of unpretentious
sorts (he boasted that he'd concocted his first movie scenario
while on the toilet), and he wanted a conspirator nearby, someone with whom he could share the wealth in every sense. Of all
his sharply cynical friends, Hecht seemed most suited to this

With Sara, Manky, and Rose, Coney Island

line of work. A fast and fluent writer, he was a so-called pro, but he wouldn't, Mankiewicz knew, take this strangely lucrative gig too seriously. Meanwhile, they could enjoy themselves as they laughed at the whole enterprise together, and in their own particular ham-on-Jewish-wry style. The two shared an exuberantly taboo-smashing sense of humor which they'd trotted out for public consumption in a short-lived, jokey New York tabloid, *The Low Down*, whose opening issue in May 1925 blared that "VULGARITY IS THE GREATEST AMERICAN ART." Modeled loosely on Hecht's *Chicago Literary Times*, this "Magazine That Bites in The Clinches, Catches Flies in Church and Whistles At The Molls On Main Street" had a much stronger Yiddish accent than its midwestern forebear, complete with various Fanny

Brice–esque ditties attributed to one Alfred Pupick (student), "Why Yenta Had Her Shoes Re-soled," "Who Will Protect the Woiking Goil, or The Tragedy From a Socialist Picnic," and "Oi Yenta, Oi My Yenta!" (This "Pome from a Broken Heart End a Lost Herring" starts: "My Yenta had ah nose det looked / Just like ah loaf from bread. / End—ah smell from Gorgonzola / Henged alvays round her head.") The line connecting this early Mankiewicz-Hecht creation to the various Marx Brothers movies they'd both eventually help chortle into existence was a short and snappy one.

Mankiewicz's invitation may finally have lured him west, but Hecht had been flirting with the movies for some time, if from a studied remove: attraction and aversion would always mingle in uneasy measure when it came to Hecht and Hollywood. As far back as 1915, Theodore Dreiser had suggested to Hecht that they start a production company together, since the movies were, according to the Chicago novelist, "going to take the place of literature in the U.S.A., and fortunes were going to be made out of them." Hecht's editors at the *Journal* had warned him against "succumb[ing] to any such get-rich-quick scheme"—"good advice," as Hecht later put it, "though poor prophecy." The same year, he sent a story idea to an up-and-coming actor he'd met in Chicago, one Douglas Fairbanks, who'd passed it on to the plucky young screenwriter Anita Loos (she said Hecht had "flippantly scrawled" his plot "on the back of a used envelope"). Working under D. W. Griffith, she turned these few lines into a successful silent, *Double Trouble*, whose suicidal yet cowardly hero hires a gang of mobsters to kill him. In that instance Hecht seems to have been drawn to the cinema's comedic possibilities, but an aphoristic column he'd dashed off for *Screenland* magazine in 1924 gave a taste of his already-tart take on the more hackneyed aspects of the medium: "My composite memory of all the movies I have seen," he wrote, still hunkered down near Lake Michigan, "is that of a lady, suffering from adenoids, about to be ravished by an unshaven fellow in a Mackinaw. Dimly, on the outskirts of this tableau, I seem to see a dog sled, a gentleman in a checked suit offering somebody a cigar, and over it all a sentence reading, 'With hearts a-tremble they turned their faces to the new day.'"

Soon after Hecht pulled in to New York, he had grown close to the ambitious son of a bankrupted East Coast movie tycoon, David O. Selznick, who was then in his early twenties and wavering between a career in the movies and one in literature. Hecht was, according to Selznick's biographer David Thomson, the idealistic producer-to-be's "first significant friend" and Selznick, nine years Hecht's junior, looked up to him in a slightly awestruck way—admiring the older writer's dashing black suit and ribbon tie, and describing him in a letter as "a great mental stimulus . . . eccentric, possibly, and radical; but one needn't share his views to appreciate the Brain of the man. Brains and humor: these have Hecht, and how many sins one can forgive a possessor of the two." For two thousand dollars, he commissioned Hecht to write him a novel (it would have marked Selznick's debut as publisher), and Hecht dashed off several drafts, but since he was, he told Selznick, "selling scenarios right and left" to various studios—which scenarios these were isn't indicated—he seems to have been too busy to buckle down and finish. In 1925, a New York playwright friend asked Hecht to travel to Florida to help him rework a script for matinee idol Thomas Meighan. Hecht agreed, even as he contended, "Anybody with a good memory for clichés and unafraid to write like a child can bat out a superb movie in a few days." Be that as it may, the pair got distracted by various dubious real estate and publicity schemes, and the picture, like the novel for Selznick, never materialized.

All these cinematic trial balloons had amounted to little more than dabbling, but the telegraphic offer from Mankiewicz to pick up and come to the coast on Paramount's dime was something else altogether. More than the promise of easy money or steady employment, it seemed, at a particularly low point in Hecht's writerly evolution, an enticing creative challenge, an adventure.

Not that he would ever *admit* to that allure or to his own eagerness to try his hand at a new form. If anything, he made a point from the very outset of denouncing what he considered the idiocy of the film industry—and of insisting how simple it was to throw together a script. Although he'd seen, he maintained, "no more than a dozen movies," within his first four days in town that December he had heard "all that was to be known about the flickers." Mankiewicz explained matter-of-factly that in a movie "the hero, as well as the heroine, has to be a virgin. The villain can lay anybody he wants, have as much fun as he wants cheating and stealing, getting rich and whipping the servants. But you have to shoot him in the end." Hecht instead resolved to "skip the heroes and heroines, to write a movie containing only villains and bawds. I would not have to tell any lies then."

According to another account (as always, there were multiple, morphing versions) Hecht claimed that he'd arrived in Hollywood without "the faintest idea of what a movie was or how to write one" when he happened to spot in the lobby of the Beverly Wilshire Hotel a man who had been a stool pigeon for the Chicago state's attorney when Hecht worked that beat. After swapping stories with this former informant about various gangsters and "murdering rascals of renown," he knew the movie he wanted to write. Dashed off in less than a week ("exactly," he sneered, as he'd spend a few hours drafting a magazine short story he "wouldn't care to sign"), Hecht's scenario would serve as the ground for that penumbral masterpiece *Underworld*, directed as a kind of soundless tone poem—all dark streets, falling feathers, swirling streamers, and puffs of expressive smoke—by a difficult Vienna-born Jew named Jonas Sternberg, a.k.a.

Josef von Sternberg. Besides resuscitating von Sternberg's career after several stillborn or aborted projects, *Underworld* was the first gangster movie to appeal to a wide audience and the first picture to garner Hecht acclaim for his screenwriting. Even at this stage, though, he professed little more than pucker-faced distaste for the entire undertaking.

He'd been happy to pocket the ten thousand dollars offered him by the studio bosses after he read them his eighteen-page story, "full of moody Sandburgian sentences." And it had pleased him to sign a yearlong contract to write another four scenarios, even as he left town for New York, a *Variety* headline proclaiming "Ben Hecht, Coast Success." But he said that on first seeing *Underworld*, he felt he would vomit. The "half-dozen sentimental touches" added by von Sternberg were the apparent cause of his nausea, and Hecht demanded that his name be removed from the credits—which was easier said than done. While von Sternberg may since have been lauded as "a lyricist of light and shadow" by film critic Andrew Sarris and been widely recognized as one of the great auteurs, at the time, he was struggling to find his place in Hollywood and had been assigned late to the movie as a substitute for the original director, Arthur Rosson. Hecht's own name seemed to mean a good deal more to the Paramount publicity machine than did the director's. In the buildup to the picture's release, von Sternberg's role in it all was only occasionally mentioned, while the industry papers and fan magazines referred with excitement to the forthcoming "Ben Hecht thriller," "the Ben Hecht story," or simply "Ben Hecht's 'Underworld.'"

Hecht wasn't just being ornery in refusing credit for a film that may be brilliant but which bears a decidedly peculiar textural and tonal relation to the words he'd set down on paper. His written story and the finished film seem in fact like night and day—literally. Hecht's hard-boiled scenario unfolds in the glare of stark morning light, starting sharply—"A million alarm

clocks were ringing in a million bedrooms. The city was waking up and rubbing the sleep out of its eyes"—while von Sternberg's darkly romantic tour de force of a film opens in the hushed,
nocturnal realm of dreams, its initial credit announcing, "A
great city in the dead of night—streets lonely, moon-flooded—
buildings empty as the cliff-dwellings of a forgotten age."

Hecht's contribution, though, was major, and more broadly
conceptual, in that he provided the movie with its gritty yet
somehow glamorous subject: small-time gangsters and their
pouting molls, their bacchanalian revelries and brutal street
warfare. We might even say he provided *the movies* with this
subject, since *Underworld* set forth the raw materials for nearly
a century of gangster dramas-to-come, from Hecht's own script
for *Scarface* and right on through the *Godfathers*, Scorsese, and
The Sopranos. While *Underworld* wasn't technically the first gang-
land movie, it animated for the first time the rich and surprisingly compelling array of shady characters at work in this nether-
realm beyond the law, and this too seems Hecht's handiwork.
Having spent a good deal of his time as a journalist reporting
on genuine criminals, he was able to articulate the distinctions
among them, to feel for them even at their most depraved, and
in doing so to give Hollywood both a fresh vocabulary, of "nifty
dressers and dopes, bouncers, shicks, bawds, forgers, safe blow-
ers, stickup men and wiretappers," and a wide new sympathetic
range. Hecht conceived the vivid triangle at the film's center—
thuggish Bull Weed, his knowing flapper girlfriend Feathers,
and his intellectual sidekick, with a "gentleman's face and . . .
manners." (In Hecht's story he's named Weasel and in the movie,
Rolls Royce, otherwise known as Clive Brook.) And he also
furnished the picture with its setting, described in his very literary scenario as "the huge tossing mechanism of steel, smoke
and stone; of windows, of lusts, derbies, despairs and hallelujahs
identified on the maps as Chicago." In the movie that backdrop
is unnamed but obvious if also abstracted into a free-floating

Evelyn Brent as Feathers McCoy, *Underworld*

phantasmagoria of dim soundstage alleys and spooky speak-
easies. Von Sternberg was no documentarian, yet in a way the
power of the finished film lies in precisely the tug-of-war—or
meeting place—between his sensibility and Hecht's. The writer
was a brassy tough-talker, the director a brooding painter of
specters and shades. Both were cynics of soft-centered sorts.
The ironic billboard that looms over Bull Weed in one of the
film's early scenes, promising "THE CITY IS YOURS," appears to
have been von Sternberg's own touch, though Hecht's story offers an image that anticipates it, however crudely, as Bull Weed
"raised his eyes to the sky," and "there was a wind blowing a
plume of factory smoke into a strange design . . . the design of
a noose."

While still in the works, the movie was advertised by Paramount as among "the most important features of the coming year," though after seeing the finished version, the skittish producers apparently had a change of heart, with one of the studio's founders, Jesse Lasky, describing it as "so sordid and savage in content, so different from accepted film fare" that they almost shelved it. But when the picture opened unannounced at a single Times Square theater in August 1927, word of something exciting trickled out. Within three hours the place was mobbed as a huge crowd tried to push its way into the movie house, which then stayed open all night to accommodate the hordes. The critics not only celebrated this "whale of a film yarn . . . the big wow generally"—they attributed its power in large part to Hecht, whose "underworld acquaintance with the Cicero and South Side gun mob" had injected the movie with a thrilling dose of real-life frisson.

Credit for a runaway hit might have pleased another man, yet even when Hecht won the first-ever Academy Award for original story for *Underworld* in 1929, he continued to growl and pronounce himself "outraged." The idea of "receiving a prize for this piece of good hack work was annoying," he later explained, with what may actually be a touch of self-mockery, "because I was a man of letters." He returned the Oscar with an indignant telegram snarling his refusal to be honored by Hollywood, which he considered "an outhouse on the Parnassus." He did think the Academy's president, Douglas Fairbanks, "a very nice fellow," however, so when the heavy, gold-plated bronze statuette was quietly returned to him, he agreed to hang on to it. It would, he conceded, make an excellent doorstop.

Never mind that 1968 estimation of Jean-Luc Godard's that Hecht was "a genius" who "invented 80 percent of what is used in Hollywood movies today." Hecht had his own take on the movies—"one of the bad habits that corrupted our century," he called them in 1954: "an eruption of trash that has lamed the American mind and retarded Americans from becoming a cultured people."

How to square Hecht's major achievement as a screenwriter with his major contempt for film and all it entailed? Why his compulsion not just to bite the Hollywood hand that fed him, but to shred it with his teeth?

Was the gap between his mastery and his mockery another of Hecht's attention-grabbing gambits—a mere pose? He seemed really to mean his disdain. And it wasn't a matter of false modesty: Hecht's notoriously low opinion of the medium through which he'd risen to the loftiest heights was too dark, too total for that to make sense. And while other literary writers transplanted to the studios certainly shared his frustration at the compromises demanded of them in this sunny, shallow context, he was far more outspoken about it than others, and he was relentless in his critique. Could it have been self-hatred— gut-level disgust at his own preternatural facility with words, with plots, with dramatic set pieces? That doesn't seem right either, as Hecht's ego was hardly wanting. Was it mistrust of authority? Of consensus? Writing a successful Hollywood picture meant, almost by definition, capitulation to producers and to some vague idea of "the popular taste." Long before he'd ever caught sight of a single palm tree, Hecht had often seized hold of an extreme position and brandished it to upset those in power, or to spite self-declared guardians of good taste. Then again, maybe he was simply hitting back at the generally boorish bosses who didn't bother to hide their antipathy toward writers—"Schmucks with Underwoods," as Jack Warner (one of the Brothers) is said to have dubbed them.

At the peak of his movie career, Hecht was known as Hollywood's highest-paid screenwriter—he commanded as much as $125,000 for less than a month's work in the midst of the Great

Depression and at a time when the average studio writer earned approximately $120 a week—though, if anything, the outlandish size of his paychecks seemed only to further stoke his wrath. In a comically blistering "Prayer to His Bosses" that he published in samizdat fashion during this period, he let rip his deep, almost delighted, ingratitude toward the executives who controlled the studio purse strings, and, by extension, his own labor. It begins: "Good gentlemen who overpay/Me fifty times for every fart,/Who hand me statues when I bray/And hail my whinnying as Art—/I pick your pockets every day/But how you bastards break my heart."

And here, with that heartbreak, we may be getting closer to grasping what so agitated Hecht about the deal he'd made with these devils in their fancy double-breasted suits. "Writing cheaply, writing falsely, writing with 'less' than you have, is a painful thing," he'd admit when his whimsical mood had faded. The riches available to him in Hollywood came at a steep price: they depended on his willingness to check his own lofty sense of writerly vocation at the moguls' office doors.

> Good gentlemen, I only trace
> With cautious word the horrid chore,
> The tribulation that I face
> In playing literary whore—
> That little nuance of disgrace
> That one gets so much money for . . .
>
> Yet hear my prayer—the timid plea
> That trickles from my venal bed,
> The echo of integrity
> That still wails in my empty head.
> Attend! And please don't fire me
> For not being altogether dead.

The irony is that Hecht was among the very worst judges of his own talents. His novels, his stories are effective enough—

sharply observed, clever, and eloquent at their best—but with the passage of time, they frankly seem like trifling period pieces. Aside from his dutiful biographer, who these days reads *Humpty Dumpty, The Kingdom of Evil, The Champion from Far Away*? Hecht's movies, on the other hand, include some of the most enduring ever made. Even if we count just those films on which his name appears, the list is ridiculous for its range and its quality and includes, among many others, *Scarface, Design for Living, Topaze, Viva Villa!, Twentieth Century, Crime Without Passion, The Scoundrel, Barbary Coast, Nothing Sacred, Gunga Din, Wuthering Heights, It's a Wonderful World, Angels over Broadway, Comrade X, Lydia, Tales of Manhattan, Spellbound, Notorious, Kiss of Death, Monkey Business, A Farewell to Arms*, and so on and amazingly on. Although he isn't credited with the script, *His Girl Friday* owes its five-miles-a-minute *Front Page*–derived dialogue and its deliriously newsprint-drunk soul to Hecht (and MacArthur) as much as it does director Howard Hawks or screenwriter Charles Lederer, a protégé of Hecht's with whom he worked behind the scenes on the movie. The Pulitzer Prize–winning playwright Sydney Howard is the single writer whose name is emblazoned on the flowery Technicolor credits of *Gone with the Wind*, but some fourteen others also pitched in, including Hecht, who it seems (accounts differ) whipped the movie's first nine reels into shootable shape over the course of seven frantic eighteen-hour days spent in banana-and-peanut-fueled seclusion with the film's final director, Victor Fleming, and its obsessive producer and mastermind, Hecht's old friend David Selznick. When Hecht was called in at the last minute as a kind of emergency-room script doctor, he hadn't read the fat best seller by Margaret Mitchell on which the movie was based. With no time to spare—the picture was already well into costly production—Fleming and his boss acted out the parts while Hecht lay on the couch and took in what must have been the remarkable spectacle of the very Jewish, very boyish David O.

Selznick batting his eyelashes and fiddle-dee-deeing as Scarlett O'Hara.

While Hecht's best movies are marked by his touch—glib wit and knowing insouciance are often present, as are romantic triangles and jaded reporters—ascribing credit to him for a given film's imaginative essence is, as with all Hollywood products of this era, a tenuous enterprise. High-flown questions of *auteur* vs. author aside, when it came to screenwriting during much of this period, official credit was granted only to those who contributed more than 50 percent of a film's dialogue, a steep prospect in the context of a studio system that produced pictures if not quite according to the Gothic cathedral model then at least in the detached manner of a Detroit car assembly line. (Hecht himself likened the notion of "speak[ing] personally through a movie" to "trying to speak through a stone wall.") In his case, attribution may be even more precarious than usual since "the Hecht legend," as Richard Corliss puts it, "assures that any attempt at a comprehensive filmography will be both incomplete and overly generous. That Hecht worked uncredited on many films is unquestioned; that he left many other projects to be developed by members of the 'School of Hecht' is just as certain." (Soon after establishing himself in Hollywood, Hecht hired a small stable of younger writers to work with him at what was generally known as his "script factory," where the collective would sometimes bear down on multiple screenplays at once. Still, estimates of how much writing he farmed out may also be inflated as, according to one of the laborers in that "factory," an aspiring playwright and former copywriter named John Lee Mahin, "To try to do Ben's work for him [was] silly. . . . I'd try to work and he'd say, 'No, no' and then he'd sit down and rattle off something.") However one tallies the final count, it's clear that there were numerous other celebrated movies that he ghostwrote, tweaked, scripted pseudonymously, or to which he added some critical component—from *A Star Is Born* to *Angels* with *Dirty Faces, Stagecoach, The Shop Around the Corner, Foreign Correspondent, Duel in the Sun, The Paradine Case, Strangers on a Train,* and *Roman Holiday*—to say nothing of the dozens of B or B-ish movies on which he also worked without fanfare.

Meanwhile—this too is without doubt—he helped to concoct or refine entire genres, not just the gangster film but the newspaper picture, the action movie, the noir, the historical epic, the screwball comedy. Hecht's contributions to that form in particular were substantial. Many of his own real-life antics played out in this zone—quick-witted, sexed-up, verbally carbonated—and it came naturally to him to bring that air of frenetic, suggestive japery he so enjoyed to the page, bound for the screen.

Miriam Hopkins, Fredric March, Gary Cooper, *Design for Living*

Sam Jaffe, Cary Grant, Victor McLaglen, Douglas Fairbanks Jr., *Gunga Din*

He also added in ways large and small to the accomplishments of Alfred Hitchcock, Otto Preminger, Ernst Lubitsch, John Ford, and Orson Welles, as well as von Sternberg and, especially, Hawks—whose oeuvre is inextricably bound up with Hecht's; so too Allan Dwan, Lewis Milestone, William Wellman, King Vidor, Charles Vidor, William Wyler, Julien Duvivier, Henry Hathaway, Victor Fleming, Harry D'Arrast, Jack Conway, George Stevens, Robert Montgomery . . . all told, much of the directorial pantheon of Golden Age Hollywood, from its major Olympians to its minor deities. Not to mention those more or less mortal Marx Brothers, frolicking amid the muses.

His was not, in other words, the case of a Faulkner or a Fitzgerald, a Huxley or a Brecht brought low or kept from his true calling by screenwriting. Screenwriting *was* Hecht's calling, whether he liked it or not.

But the ticklish truth was that while he claimed loudly to loathe the movies and all they stood for, he also quietly adored them—relishing as he did the rollicking context in which they came to life. More than that, as he admitted in a 1944 book that only parenthetically concerns the boomtown to which Manky's telegram had drawn him that fateful winter of 1926, he "fell in love with Hollywood" the first night he spent in it.

And how could he not have? "Here in this city engaged in making a toy that was already sweeping the world clean of Mah Jong sets, yoyo sticks, and lonely evenings," he found "everything and everybody—great thinkers, mighty swindlers, phantasts astride dreams as spavined as Rosinante, artists falling down stairs, poets screaming for help (I saw one catch fire in a fireplace seven feet high), millionaires who had not yet had time for a shave . . ."

"I have written many stories about Hollywood and made much fun of its clap-trap splendors," he confessed. "I have criticized its whirligig castrations of the Arts, its triumphs over sanity, and its coronation of buncombe. But in nearly all I have written there has been a lie of omission. I neglected to say that all these things I loved. How can you help doting on a town so daft, so dizzy, so sizzling; a town tumbling with the alarms and delights of a fairy tale book?"

Indeed. While this sudden avowal of ardor for the setting he'd spent so much energy lambasting may seem a contradiction, it also stands to reason of a perversely Hechtian sort. There are perhaps shades here of the charged dynamic between the Cary Grant and Rosalind Russell characters in *His Girl Friday*. Bitterly divorced and tussling cattily yet still so obviously in love, editor Walter Burns and reporter Hildy Johnson may be at each other's throats, but they also have each other's numbers—

Cary Grant, Ralph Bellamy, Rosalind Russell, *His Girl Friday*

as in a sense Hollywood had Hecht's, and vice versa. Whatever his scorn for producers (whose chief task was, he said, "turning good writers into movie hacks") and for many of the hired hands around him (of a hundred people churning out scripts, he counted "possibly five who could write a legible letter"), Hecht was also enchanted by the opera buffa lunacy of the place. Like the Chicago of his early newspaper years and Berlin right after the war, Hollywood of the late twenties and thirties was bursting with larger-than-life characters and a wide-open sense of possibility, wildness, even absurdity. The vast sums to be racked up quickly gave moviemaking the air of a high rollers' craps game played with funny money. "You were," Hecht would write of himself at this stage, "a sort of literary errand boy with an oil magnate's income." Meanwhile, you were—

93

he was—surrounded by "witty and superior folk," and a party seemed always to be popping up somewhere: Hecht claimed that within his first few hours in town, Robert Benchley and the Yale-educated humorist Donald Ogden Stewart arrived at his office bearing gin bottles and didn't budge for several sodden days. In a letter to Rose from one of his initial Hollywood stints, he recounted that, the night before, he'd "circulated among the gilt and tinsel of the town, the occasion being a formal shindig thrown by Chevalier Mankiewicz—a fete with butlers, dress suits, salami, punch bowls, etcetera. The event was in Our Honor, we being the Guests to be met."

Other times, such spontaneity and stiffness converged, as on a different evening—a few years after Hecht began commuting between Hollywood and Nyack, where he and Rose had bought a rambling old treasure chest of a house right over the water—Mankiewicz exerted "hydraulic pressure insistence" and persuaded Hecht and MacArthur to let his chauffeur drive them to a party at the home of actress Ina Claire. (MacArthur had also taken up work in Hollywood and would soon—as they'd resolved during that fateful picnic a few years before—buy a place in Nyack. No matter how much time they spent elsewhere, together or apart, the hilly Hudsonside town remained the home to which they would both return and remain devoted till the end of their days. They lived "about a football field apart" from each other, according to Hecht, and shared a little boat they named *The Anchovy*, on which they spent long raucous afternoons sailing and goofing around.) At Claire's they found "the usual group of refugees, all huddled in a room full of Murillo's, Ribera's, Titian's and other works of art." Among others, Harpo was there: "It is almost impossible to go anywhere without finding Harpo." But there was no food in the house, so Claire and some sixteen of her guests wound up crashing the dinner party next door, at the grand seaside mansion of another actress, Marion Davies, mistress of William Randolph Hearst, also present.

In what sounds like a draft of a scene from the as-yet-unwritten Mankiewicz script for *Citizen Kane*, Hecht described for Rose the "huge room about 125 feet long—all English, with four dining tables in it and magnificent walnut walls, red brocaded drapes—real opulence." In another room "there was enough food for 200 people. . . . 100 lobsters, 20 pounds of sturgeon (lax), hundreds of pounds of turkey. I stared at these viands which would have gone utterly to waste hadn't our seventeen extra mouths come in and which anyway were more than half wasted—and I realized that that is the way Marion lives every day. That food always lies in state on her serving table—enough for fifty guests. . . . That if guests come, good. If they don't the food is probably thrown out. This impressed me more than the hostess."

Hecht's attitude toward this extravagance and toward the glitterati with whom he now rubbed pretty shoulders usually swerved between chuckling wonder and detached disgust. "I have never been so vastly bored in years as since I landed here," he yawned to Rose in another letter. "I had almost forgot that it is people who bore one not solitude. All the celebrities here—they come a dime a dozen—all heading for the camera like a lot of guests at a Polish wedding." While he was surrounded by various kindred spirits, he claimed in his account of the lavish dinner at Davies's that Hearst was "the first person I met in Hollywood who remotely interested me" and scathingly described some of the other partygoers, including "a reddish faced, greasy mouthed, popping eyed Joan Crawford, a Monjou [Adolphe Menjou] looking like a limp balloon."

Hecht was a regular at such soirées—"my slightly bawdy talk and irresponsible mental manners somewhat astonish and attract"—and would later recall with fondness the "vivid people, long and noisy luncheons, nights of gaiety and gambling, hotel suites and rented palaces overrun with friends, partners, secretaries and happy servants." Some of the vivid people enjoying nights of gaiety with him in those hotel suites were, of course, women. His frequent declarations of longing for Rose's caresses notwithstanding, Hecht was, according to Mahin, "almost childlike" in his need to "get . . . involved and embroiled." Howard Hawks said that he "loved being a Romeo" and called him, with a laugh, "a pretty devious guy." In his letters to Rose from Hollywood, Hecht alternated between swearing, for instance, that "I haven't even noticed the color of a pair of female eyes since I left yours. . . . My God, I doubt if I could even feel normal touching a strange woman," and offering long, self-flagellating pleas for forgiveness for unspecified but apparently sexual transgressions. He alluded euphemistically to his "carryings on" and his "weakness," as he both bemoaned "the need of my juvenile nerves for stimulants" and assured her that "to you my doings are seemingly more important than me—even though they are doings I can't remember."

For all his extramarital entanglements, it seems he found the most meaningful and lasting companionship at work. That was the magnet that had pulled him to California in the first place and the force that always sustained him. And despite his disdain for what he saw as the sham aspects of filmmaking, he was enough of a cheerful cynic to know he too had a role to play in the act—"All the mumbling and eye rolling and all the intellectual travail of story conferences . . . make you feel that the Movies are the dementia praecox ward of literature," he wrote Rose in yet another letter. "I'm not mad at Hollywood or out of step with it. Your little boy remains as adjustable as a zipper."

Hecht was at his most content when engaged in what he called "the camaraderie of collaboration," especially with his male friends. (He and Rose had written a few plays together around 1926–27, though only one, the farcical *Man-Eating Tiger*, made it to the stage. It closed in Philadelphia to lukewarm reviews—"utter lunacy . . . just about one man in 20 likes this kind of theatrical entertainment," according to *Variety*. And while she remained deeply involved in all his nonmovie writing, serving as what Hecht called "the keeper of my logic, editor of my reiterations and vanguard of all my critics," that play was their last official literary team effort since, as Rose put it, "I preferred our marriage to collaboration.") Meanwhile, the "pleasant anonymity" of film work—the dozens of technicians involved in production, his ostensible indifference to screen credit—brought out the generosity and freewheeling best in him. His ego wasn't at stake here as it was when he devoted himself to a novel. And unlike the lonely business of literary composition, scriptwriting took place in a busy, rowdy, improvisatory setting that fed his warmer, less self-important instincts. It was a lot like the newspaper's local room: "You wrote with the phone ringing like a firehouse bell, with the boss charging in and out of your atelier, with the director grimacing and grunting in an adjoining armchair." Over the course of the twenty or so visits he paid to Hollywood across the decades, each trip lasting from several weeks to a few months, he worked in this three-ring-circus fashion, often living or spending most of his waking hours with his collaborators—with MacArthur, with Gene Fowler, with Mahin and the other "factory" workers, with various directors, and sometimes with Lederer, the half-Irish, half-Jewish nephew of Marion Davies, who had, as Hecht enthused on first making his acquaintance, "pointed teeth, pointed ears, is . . . completely bald and stands on his head a great deal."

Despite his initial insistence on the proverbial piece of cake that Hecht considered screenwriting, he later altered that assertion and described it as no easier than "good writing." In fact, "it's just as hard to make a toilet seat as it is a castle window. But the view is different." Were Hecht himself to script this period, we might now be treated to a quick montage—shots of Ben and Charlie hard at work and play in and around the enormous Culver City house where they'd installed themselves in late 1930. Situated on an avocado ranch overlooking the

MGM lot and a hundred oil wells, the house soon became the scene of a nearly perpetual party. Hecht later recalled one typical evening there, in the course of which everyone from Ernst Lubitsch to Dashiell Hammett, Jean Harlow to Hawks and the ubiquitous Harpo drank themselves silly. How did they manage to get any work done? Sober or sloshed, somehow they did. Hecht and MacArthur had come west this time to write a lucrative bit of Orientalist fluff for producer Sam Goldwyn, *The Unholy Garden*, which would feature Ronald Colman ambling elegantly in white linen across a soundstage Sahara (not much of a film)—though they had designs on holing up at the ranch, amid the Japanese pines, to finish the third act of their new play, *Twentieth Century*, which together with Hawks they would soon transform into one of the most gloriously screwy of all screwball comedies. In the film version John Barrymore hams his happy way through the role of Oscar Jaffe, a fire-breathing dragon of a theatrical producer, and Carole Lombard kicks and flounces, pouts and giggles quite delightfully in her first major comic role, as the two-bit-actress whom Jaffe turns, Svengali-style, into Broadway star Lily Garland, formerly known as Mildred Plotka.

But before that celebration of fakery, slang, high-end train travel, pale silk pajamas, and shameless scenery-chewing came another groundbreaking Hawks-Hecht production, *Scarface*. As is often the case with a film deemed "classic," so many contradictory accounts of its creation exist, determining who deserves credit for what becomes not just hard but futile. Was it Hawks who initiated this project, talking a reluctant Hecht into working on the picture—or could the choice of screenwriter have come from the eccentric millionaire oilman and producer Howard Hughes, who was, according to Hecht, "lurking like a deaf octopus in a wood-paneled room" when they first met? (Hughes had already bought the screen rights to *The Front Page* and would produce Lewis Milestone's kinetic film version the next year.) Or was Hecht's role in writing *Scarface* engineered by his then

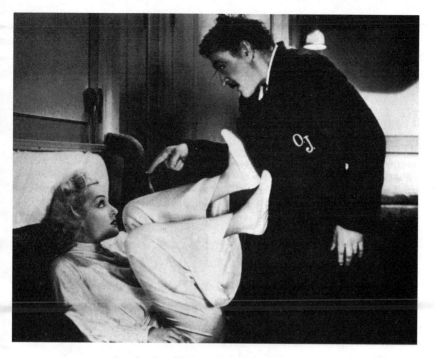

Lombard and Barrymore, *Twentieth Century*

slightly desperate novice agent Leland Hayward, who claimed to have "conned" his way into Hughes's lair and cajoled him into hiring Hecht? While Hecht wrote in his memoirs that David Selznick's hustling older brother Myron had been his agent then, it was Hayward who, years on, recalled arriving at Hughes's office to collect the thousand dollars the producer had agreed to pay Hecht in cash every day at 5 P.M. Hayward also conjured the scene of Hecht typing furiously as he, the beleaguered go-between, delivered a pile of bills and pleaded with him, "Ben—please—*slow down!*" According to legend, Hecht banged out the script in eleven days—or was it nine? Fourteen? In correspondence from the period, Hecht mentions nothing about the pay-per-day arrangement and writes simply: "Hughes offered me ten grand for a week's work on Scar Face. I'm doing it as homework when I'm not with Goldwynn [*sic*]."

More substantively: was the unspoken but palpable sexual bond between squat yet hulking Tony "Scarface" Camonte and his slinky sister Cesca originally Hawks's idea, or Hecht's? Hawks always insisted he'd been the one to suggest transplanting the incestuous story of the Borgia siblings to latter-day Chicago—though Mahin, who also worked on the script, contended that the Renaissance twist had been Hecht's. ("*Ben* said that to *Hawks*. I heard him say that," Mahin maintained, decades after the fact. The Borgias were Hecht's "favorite characters," while "Howard, bless his heart, probably knew who they were, but I think he looked them up in the encyclopedia.") And who first suggested that the former Yiddish stage actor Paul Muni, previously known as Muni Weisenfreund, be brought in from New York to play Camonte? Who instructed George Raft to flip a coin menacingly whenever he appeared? Was the film's startling brutality the product of Hecht's own hardened views— toward both violence and the vox populi? "I killed as many people as I could shoot down," he'd later brag of this script. "I knew audiences adored disaster, sudden death, explosions, much more than they did ideas, points of view." Or did the film's rough energy and high body count mount later, as Hughes and Hawks squared off against Hollywood's moralizer-in-chief, Will Hays, lead enforcer of the fledgling Production Code? The industry's own "decency" guidelines, first set forth in 1927, the Code was meant to prohibit or severely limit onscreen everything from profanity, drug-trafficking, nudity, and "ridicule of the clergy" to white slavery, miscegenation, the "use of fire arms," sedition, "surgical operations," "brutality and possible gruesomeness," "sympathy for criminals," "excessive or lustful kissing," and "theft, robbery, safe-cracking, and dynamiting of trains, mines, buildings, etc. (having in mind the effect which a too-detailed description of these may have upon the moron)."

Paul Muni, *Scarface*

Hays's harrumphing deputies had declared the movie, when still in script form, "the most harsh and frank gangster picture we have ever had" and warned, "If you should be foolhardy enough to make *Scarface*, this office will make certain it is never released." To this stern admonition Hughes responded with a memo to Hawks: "Screw the Hays Office. Start the picture and make it as realistic, as exciting, as grisly as possible." And that was really just the beginning of their war with the censors: the film was released only in 1932, nearly a year after it was shot, with various cuts and additions and with *"Shame of a Nation"* tacked on to the title, as a kind of prudish p.s.

For all these concessions, throughout his life, Hawks would call *Scarface* one of his favorite pictures, and the critics would tend to agree that it was among his—and Hecht's—best, though Hecht would typically dismiss it as "a cheapy film." He did, however, enjoy and appreciate Hawks himself—and described him to Rose soon after they began working together as "charming . . . one of the few half humans—to whom movies are a pleasant sideline, a thing to be done as work, not to be lived as a career."

It was a curious description of a man then in the process of becoming one of the greatest American directors of all time. But in fact the statement says more about Hecht and his own sense of the movies—and of careers—than it does about Howard Hawks.

As does the dynamic final shot of the uncensored version of *Scarface*. The authorship of this image, too, is not entirely traceable, though it's tempting to read it as a dark inside joke, a mordant memo, perhaps, from Ben Hecht to himself. The conceit is borrowed from *Underworld* but now raised several powers—as the camera pans up from the twisted, bullet-riddled corpse of Tony Camonte to a sign that glows "THE WORLD IS YOURS," at once a boast and threat.

6

The Rogues

HECHT COULD BEAR Hollywood only in small doses, and when he left town to head back east, he seemed intent on flushing all thoughts of hackwork from his system. While the place exerted a certain emotional hold on him even from a distance—his parents had moved to Los Angeles in the late 1920s, and Rose periodically set out alone for the California studios, where beginning in the early 1930s she took up a series of short-term writing assignments—that hold had little to do with the movies. The almost daily letters he scribbled her from his wood-paneled, book-filled Nyack study during these separations spill with lusty encomia to her breasts, her laughter, her "approbation"—but scripts themselves (his, hers) go almost completely unmentioned.

He was, as it happens, busy trying during these Hudson-side stints to redeem his own words and their literary value. He was writing a novel. Whether deliberately or not, he was also disgorging onto its pages some of his blackest and most per-

verse thinking ever, as if, perhaps, to counter the ostensibly
amiable give-and-take of those humiliating West Coast story
conferences. The result was a book that is highly problematic
—misanthropic and confused—though at the same time one
too weirdly provocative in its perspective and too occasionally
dazzling in its prose to be dismissed out of hand. If not as an
exemplary literary object then as a telling biographical document, *A Jew in Love* seems a critical piece of the puzzle that was
Ben Hecht.

"Joe Boshere (born Abe Nussbaum)," it begins,

> was a man of thirty—a dark-skinned little Jew with a vultur-
> ous and moody face, a reedy body and a sense of posture.
>
> The Jews now and then hatch a face which for Jewish-
> ness surpasses the caricatures of the entire anti-Semitic press.
> These Jew faces in which race leers and burns like some bio-
> logic disease are rather shocking to a mongrelized world.
>
> People dislike being reminded of their origins. They
> shudder a bit mystically at the sight of anyone who looks
> too much like a fish, a lizard, a chimpanzee or a Jew. This
> is probably nonsense. The Jew face is an enemy totem, an
> ancient target for spittle and, like a thing long hated, a sort
> of magic propagandist of hate . . .

And so, tauntingly, are we brought into the sordid orbit of
Boshere, New York publisher and narcissist extraordinaire, who
has contrived to invent for his own face "such unJewish expres-
sions, [and] surrounded it with such delicate mannerisms . . .
that his personality had almost lost its Semitic flavor." But for
all his assimilationist pretending, Boshere embodies the most
detestable characteristics ascribed to Jews by those who despise
them en masse. Not just a parasite, he's an actual incubus, who
spends much of the book juggling a vulgar Jewish wife, a mousy
Jewish mistress, and a strapping shiksa "dancer." He also preys
intellectually, emotionally, sexually, on his authors and their
wives: "His mental life was in the main," Hecht writes, "a pro-

cess of kleptomania." At some point in the book's relentlessly tail-chasing (in all senses) narrative, Boshere also undergoes a peculiar Jewish awakening that seems mostly about the inflation of his own ego: "He clung to race memories now, hummed Chasidic songs and sprinkled his talk with racy Yiddish epithets. . . . His shame of origin had been replaced by a desire to boast thereof. The Jewishness and immigrantism of his family had become not only the measure of his success, as with the millionaire who dotes on memories of his impoverished youth, but offered now a rich human background for his genius." Which rings a bell. Boshere has been variously identified as a stand-in for Hecht's former publisher Horace Liveright, for his Broadway producer Jed Harris, for George Jessel. The paranoia-prone Max Bodenheim assumed that Hecht was poking fun at *him* again and responded to this and to the earlier insult of *Count Bruga* with a savage satirical novel of his own, *Duke Herring*, published a few months after Hecht's latest (by Liveright, no less). In many ways, though, Joe Boshere seems to be holding a mirror up most obviously to Ben Hecht.

But how are we to take this book? Is this portrait of the Jewish arts promoter as a duplicitous young bloodsucker itself a contemptible anti-Semitic cartoon—or is it instead a not especially effective attempt to *comment on* and even deface such an unflattering portrait? Are we meant to despise Boshere or to pity him for having internalized the most grotesque stereotypes ascribed to his people? Hecht's own stance slips and slides throughout the book, and it's hard to really know whether he identifies with Boshere or finds him demonic. Both? Could this be a confession (conscious or not) of his own deeply divided sense of Jewish self? At one point, Boshere holds forth on the "slimy stranglehold of Jew consciousness" which is, he says, "the consciousness of not being a normal social human being." Yet soon after, he blasts his sister for trying to hide her Jewishness in Zionism: "To prove to the world as well as yourself that you weren't ashamed of being a Jew, what do you do? You advertise. You go in for Jewish causes. . . . In order to reconcile yourself to the simple fact that you're a Jew, you've got to go in for a large, dithering Jew Renaissance. You fill your poor little shamed mind full of Jew ideals. The Jews, you keep mumbling in your gentile accent, aren't really a grubby race of cloak and suit comics, pariahs and userers. They're a race of poets and shepherds, heroes, scholars, scientists, statesmen—beautiful souls, in short, with a socially presentable love of country."

Whatever Hecht meant to prove with this novel—and with this scorching denunciation of the very cause (and the advertising) that he himself would soon take up with an enraged vengeance—readers drew their own conclusions. His old Chicago friend Pat Covici had recently established a Manhattan publishing house with a younger partner, Donald Friede, and they had signed the book sight unseen, naming it their lead title of spring 1931. Based on Hecht's progress reports, Covici assured his colleagues that it would be "great . . . by far the best thing Hecht had ever written," and when the finished manuscript arrived, everyone at the office was, in Friede's words, "panting with excitement." Four of them began reading the book at once, passing chapters around the room, "and suddenly . . . we all stopped as if on a signal. We looked at one another and we could see that we were in agreement. We did not like the book." But instead of continuing, they marched together into Covici's office and proposed that none of them proceed further, "and we would try to forget how much we had disliked what we had already read." Since the novel had been announced in advance with fanfare, they spent the months before its release in a self-induced trance, telling each other how marvelous it was and how lucky they were to be publishing it. "We did a pretty good job," Friede writes ruefully, "of persuading ourselves." They had a book to market.

The problem wasn't that Covici and Friede were, like

Boshere, Jewish publishers in New York and that the coarse caricature hit too close to home. It displeased reviewers as well, with the *Chicago Tribune* calling it "strangely monotonous" and the *New York Times* describing it (monotonously) as "more than a bit monotonous." And the criticisms weren't only literary. Soon after the book's publication, it was denounced from the pulpit of Manhattan's Temple Rodeph Sholom by one Rabbi Louis I. Newman, who warned that "new defamers of the Jew are arising in the United States," and raged in particular against "the misrepresentations of Jewish psychology issued by reckless and indiscreet authors such as Ben Hecht. . . . 'A Jew in Love' is an atrocious malignment of the Jews."

Despite the general skepticism of the critics and its banning in Boston, Springfield, and Canada (due to swearing and sex and not, apparently, because of possible anti-Semitism), the book went on to sell nearly fifty thousand copies, making it not just a best seller but the best-selling fiction Hecht ever published. And people weren't just buying the book, they were reading and responding to its sensational contents. In a May 1931 survey of New York's City College graduating seniors (who averaged 20 years and 9 months, weighed 153 pounds, were 5 foot 8, and didn't usually drink alcohol yet favored the repeal of prohibition), Eugene O'Neill was declared the class's favorite dramatist and Albert Einstein "the greatest living man." By 297 to 201 they "decided against the practice of marrying for money." And they voted *A Jew in Love* the novel of the year.

That bitter blast of a book welled up in part from Hecht's need to wrest control back from Hollywood over his own work. His other major project of these years served a similar purpose, though it yielded much gentler results. Sometime in early 1934, Leland Hayward arranged for Hecht and MacArthur to more or less commandeer Paramount's old Eastern Service Studios in Astoria, Queens. There, over the course of the next eighteen months, they were given free rein to write, direct, and produce four movies of their own devising.

It was, for its studiocentric time, a radical idea—to put writers in charge of the final filmic product—and the quartet of Hecht-MacArthur productions that resulted from this agreement were nearly the first of their kind, predating the work of better-known writer-directors like Preston Sturges and Billy Wilder. The Hecht-MacArthur movies would also be among the earliest of American art house films—pictures that didn't hide their intellectual aspirations (or pretensions) in order to appeal to a mass audience but wore their art (or artiness) on their rolled-up sleeves.

The idea was radical in another sense as well. As Hecht claimed later, "Neither Charlie nor I had ever spent an hour on a movie set. We knew nothing of casts, budgets, schedules, booms, gobos, unions, scenery, cutting, lighting. . . . Finding ourselves with all this unknowingness in sole and lofty charge of bringing movies into existence, we were, however, not for a moment abashed." But when had they ever been abashed? If anything, they were proud of their lack of experience and flaunted it to make a point, which Hecht called "the great Secret," the fact that "90 percent of the success of a movie (or of its failure) lay in the writing of its script." Fanciful directorial gestures be damned, they'd turn on the camera, then instruct the actors to recite their lines and perform exactly as detailed the business described in the script. "A writer," according to Hecht, "if he's written any dialogue, in plays or movies, has been directing all the time on paper." This attitude was, of course, simplistic; to transfer their words to celluloid, they'd need help from a host of skilled technicians and artists—most notably, the accomplished cameraman Lee Garmes, whose credits included *Morocco*, *Shanghai Express*, and *Scarface*, and who wound up directing what he estimated was 60 to 70 percent of the first Hecht-MacArthur Astoria production, *Crime Without Passion*, and much of two other Astoria films as well. (Garmes wasn't complaining: he later described this as a "wonderful partnership.") Howard Hawks advised them briefly and Charles Lederer pitched in, as did von Sternberg's predecessor on *Underworld*, Arthur Rosson. Oscar Levant and George Antheil wrote music for these movies. The Serbian-born master of Eisensteinian montage Slavko Vorkapich was recommended to them by David Selznick as a "cutter"—an editor—but when Hecht and MacArthur realized the avant-garde *artiste* they'd taken on, they let him run wild, handing over the first three minutes of *Crime* to Vorkapich, who devised a delirious flurry of images, in which an eyeball, a gun muzzle, and a pool of blood give way to a trio of wild-haired, flowing-robed Furies cackling across the skies of New York . . . However showy and outlandish, the results—of both this sequence and the best of the Astoria movies—were often wryly inspired.

The films were also obviously the product of the willfully madcap atmosphere surrounding their creation. Helen Hayes called it "controlled chaos," while Hecht deemed this period "a two-year party that kept going seven days a week"—and it seems clear that, besides wanting to ensure their scripts reached the screen precisely as written, he and MacArthur were also determined to prove to all onlookers that, middle-aged though they were, "the boys" could still be boys. Thumbing their noses at what Hecht declared "the solemn, fat-headed productions of Hollywood," they festooned their offices with enormous Dada-ish banners emblazoned with, among other things, "CUT TO THE CHASE" and "BETTER THAN METRO ISN'T GOOD ENOUGH" (Louis B. Mayer's MGM being in those days Hollywood's chief exporter of solemn and sometimes fat-headed productions). They pasted life-sized photos of female nudes onto their office doors, with handles placed in provocative spots. Hecht paid Levant to play piano-violin duets with him between takes.

Visiting Coney Island one evening, Ben and Charlie stopped

With MacArthur, Astoria

in at the freak show and hired two microcephalic performers—
"pinheads" in the argot of the Midway—to accompany them
back to Astoria, where Bippo and Zippo were outfitted with
gray flannel suits, assigned desks, and named executive producers. According to Hecht: "Their heads used to jiggle and they
drooled a bit but they seemed to Charlie and me very much like
authentic producers." A journalist who dropped in on the set
during the filming of *Crime Without Passion* noted the "su-
perbly indifferent supervision of Ben Hecht and Charles Mac-
Arthur" and added, "It has been rumored in dark corners of
Broadway that the Messrs. Hecht and MacArthur did most of
their supervising from a recumbent position on the floor while
engaged in a heated backgammon debate." (By now the legend

of the screenwriting duo and all their hijinks was so well known that it would become something of a brand, and eventually a burden. The fun-loving team of Hollywood writers at the heart of the hit 1935 Broadway play by Bella and Sam Spewack, *Boy Meets Girl*, were apparently modeled on them. And that Katzenjammer Kids–esque depiction of their partnership drew still wider audiences and recognition when in 1938 the Spewacks turned their play into a film for Warner Brothers, with James Cagney in the spirited Ben role and the slower Pat O'Brien as a kind of thickset, dark-browed Charlie.)

But here was the real "great Secret." Despite their well-publicized Astoria shenanigans, Hecht and MacArthur were genuinely interested in making movies, and, with a little help from their friends, they managed to do that surprisingly well. Of the four films they wrote and directed between May 1934 and October 1935, two emerged as sophisticated comedic melodramas of a quirky and almost defiantly personal sort. (Both these pictures became cult classics; the second won them an Oscar for original story.) That the other two were somewhere between negligible and terrible seems not so much an indictment of their approach to moviemaking as it does a reasonable batting average. For a couple of punch-drunk amateurs, two out of four wasn't shabby.

Shot quickly on minimal budgets, with bare-bones sets, and in a mannered, static style that sometimes veered suddenly into a kind of bargain-basement Expressionism, the best of these films, *Crime Without Passion* and *The Scoundrel*, can hardly be called masterpieces, but for all their arch staginess, they're extremely entertaining. At the same time, both films seem determined to be *more* than entertaining. Both center on the sort of cynical, hyperverbal antihero who had—from *Erik Dorn* to *A Jew in Love*—been Hecht's stock in trade, if not his diabolical alter ego. Based on a short story he'd published in the *Saturday*

Evening Post, Crime stars Claude Rains as Lee Gentry, a charlatan of a New York defense attorney who goes to great, self-defeating lengths to cover up a murder. *The Scoundrel* derives from a play cowritten by Ben and Rose in the 1920s, and stars Noël Coward as Anthony Mallare, a charlatan of a New York publisher—shades of Liveright, again—who spends much of the film reveling in the role of cruelly amusing cad, but then experiences a sudden sentimental conversion when he's killed in a plane crash and his soul is condemned to wander the earth until he can find someone who'll weep at his passing.

Crime was Rains's second starring movie role and *The Scoundrel* Coward's first-ever screen appearance. And despite Hecht's insistence that a good script was the single ingredient a good movie needed, the casting of these elegant Englishmen went a long way toward making the films so shrewd. Both actors seemed born to suavely animate the roguish parts they'd been assigned and to rattle off naturally their impossibly artificial and very *written* lines. ("You comfortable little fools, sitting snug and dry in your taxidermist's window," sneers the walking-dead Mallare at a room full of all-too-human literary climbers. "So satisfied with your cackling egos, looking at life with beady eyes . . .") A general air of knowingness hovers over both movies, which brim with urbane little jokes and winking walk-ons. In *The Scoundrel*, Algonquinites Alexander Woollcott and Alice Duer Miller turn up in Mallare's waiting room, as does Lionel Stander, as the obviously Bodenheimian poet Rothenstein, smoking a corncob pipe as he deadpans acidic bons mots and florid verses. In *Crime*, Helen Hayes and Fanny Brice put in cameos, as in both films do "the boys" themselves—first as reporters then as flophouse bums.

As was often the case with Hecht's "own" work, however, he wasn't satisfied to leave quippy well enough alone. *The Scoundrel* is easily the most accomplished of the Astoria movies,

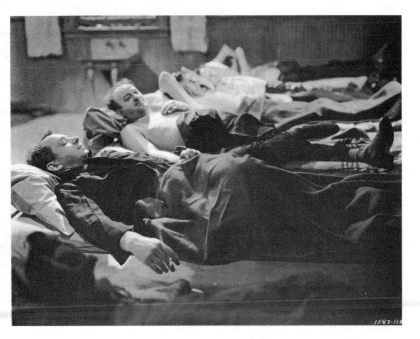

Ben and Charlie, bums

though after Mallare's death and transformation into one earnest and oddly humorless ghost, the film suffers from a mawkish straining for mystical meaning.

Coward had initially praised the story and dialogue as "marvelous" and boasted during shooting that "everyone concerned seems to think I am wonderful gorgeous superb and magnificent." He complained later, though, that he'd been "confused and irritated" throughout the entire production, and called Hecht and MacArthur's direction "erratic." But most critics enthused, with the *New York Times* describing a screening at Radio City Music Hall as "a distinctly exhilarating event," even if "regarding [the film's] merits there are likely to be many opinions, ranging the middle ground between the gentleman who stood up in his seat and shouted 'Bravo! Bravo!' and the young woman who looked around defiantly after the lights went up and made an irreverent noise with her mouth."

The other two Astoria pictures weren't much to speak of, though the neophyte writer-directors did at least manage to avoid repeating themselves. *Once in a Blue Moon* is a treacly fairy tale about Russian aristocrats who go undercover with a circus at the start of the Revolution. It was based on a story by Rose (who seemed intent on a return to her Russian beginnings, having recently translated *Uncle Vanya* for Broadway, where Jed Harris mounted a highly praised production with Lillian Gish as the glamorous young bride, Helena, and Walter Connolly in the title role). Shot mostly outdoors, near Tuxedo, New York, and starring the Vaudevillian Jimmy Savo as a little clown in an enormous suit, *Blue Moon* also features Hecht's eighteen-year-old daughter, Teddy, fair-haired and painfully stiff. With an oppressively whimsical score by Antheil, who wrote some 416 pages of accompaniment, divided into seven themes—one for Savo, one for his horse, one for his wagon, and so on—the movie doesn't have much to recommend it, relying for its putative appeal on packs of mischievously cute kids, a saccharine dream sequence, and much mugging by Savo. While it probably wasn't really "the worst picture in the world," as it was advertised by one Boston movie theater, Hecht himself admitted that he and Charlie had "forgotten the Secret" in this case. Overblown and far too precious for its own good, "our script," he declared, "was a dud."

The real dud was, though, the last of the Astoria pictures, *Soak the Rich*, which suffered from multiple ailments. A should-be zany satire about the posturing of college radicals, complete with placards hand-painted by George Grosz, the movie is unrelentingly flat—the reductio ad absurdum of Hecht's point-and-shoot directorial approach. It basically looks and sounds like a filmed play, which might have been all its creators could manage on their own (Garmes was absent this time around), but it may also have been that they'd simply grown tired of the whole adventure. A reporter visiting during the shoot described the subdued atmosphere on set: "Gone," he wrote, "are the radiant neckties." Instead, he'd encountered "a chastened pair of directors" whose new sobriety was rumored to have various possible causes. Either "the vitriolic Hecht tongue was silenced during a Paramount executive conference recently by the admonition to pay less attention to backgammon and more to picture-making," or perhaps "the frolicking Astorians couldn't stand the pace [and] found it impossible to be antic all the time."

There were, in fact, other reasons. The unfunny script was based on an unfinished play that Hecht and MacArthur had dusted off and jury-rigged to serve as a vehicle for a twenty-year-old Cecil Beaton model, making her film debut. A pouty, pretty socialite with a low voice, skinny torso, and slightly sullen bearing, Mimsi Taylor also happened to be Hecht's latest mistress. Their affair had grown much more serious than was usual for him—and her presence in his life would soon cause a major rift with Rose. Whatever this liaison meant for the Hecht marriage, it didn't do much for *Soak the Rich*. Taylor's performance is game but dilettante-ish, and Hecht's mind was clearly elsewhere.

And besides love, he had death to preoccupy him. Shortly into the film's production, a phone call came from Rose, then in Los Angeles, announcing that Hecht's parents had both been hit by a car on Wilshire Boulevard. His mother died two days later, at which Rose packed up Ben's injured father and trundled him home to Nyack. "Mother came along," remembered Hecht's brother, Pete, "in the usual baggage car."

The Astoria party was over, and so, in many ways, was an era.

7

◆━◆◆◆━◆

The Jews

In 1939, Hecht later announced, "I became a Jew and looked on the world with Jewish eyes." It was a strange claim to make. As everyone who knew him knew, he'd been a Jew from the get-go, or in fact from the ghetto where his life began—and while he'd never been even faintly religious or placed ethnicity at the center of his (ever shifting) sense of self, his Jewishness had always been there and played a part in whatever part he was playing.

But Hecht clearly meant something else, something more urgent with this full-throated declaration, and the year in question is perhaps as significant—and slippery—as the substance of his credo. Why 1939? What did he mean by "Jew"? What had come over him?

As often with Hecht, the answers involve a scramble of forces at once supremely self-involved and presciently outward-looking. The years since the Astoria experiment limped to a close had been a period of both crisis and creativity. His affair with Mimsi Taylor had almost torpedoed his marriage, as he and his elegant young mistress had decamped for Ecuador, while Rose, by her own account, "experienced as much agony as possible" and believed she'd lost him. When abroad, he started a play, *To Quito and Back*, about a washed-up, middle-aged novelist and screenwriter who decamps for Ecuador with his elegant young mistress. Though another character describes him as possessing "one of the most vicious minds in American fiction" and a notoriously dim view of Hollywood, where he has won acclaim for films like *Pancho Rides Again* (which sounds suspiciously like Hecht's *Viva Villa!*), he sees himself as a sorry has-been: "Once upon a time," he broods, "I wrote books." Torn between his mistress and the wife he has left behind, or hasn't, he comes to Quito in search of meaning, and seems driven by an unfamiliar urge to throw himself into a cause. A violent South American revolution is taking shape around them, the political particulars of which appear to matter to him less than does his desire to believe in something, anything—for the sake, perhaps, of sensation itself. He describes being among those "who understand the cries of the underdog, see through the greed and stupidity behind injustice. And who can't for the life of us feel anything. . . . Talk. Talk. Talk. We're always on the right side of discussions but never on any side of the barricades."

In the play, the writer joins the rebels and is promptly killed for his troubles. In real life, Rose won Ben back with a passionate written avowal of her faith in him, and though he ended the affair and returned home to her, those longings Hecht had expressed for some purpose grander than a "sterile, flap-doodle life of slick little greeds and slick little boasts" left a gnawing hunger.

But why should the cause have been the Jews? Why not Communism, Socialism, or—in 1937, the year *Quito* opened in New York to devastating reviews—the Spanish Civil War? Some of Hecht's allegedly newfound Jewish awareness came, no doubt, from Rose. In the years right after he broke with the very WASPy Mimsi, Hecht seemed intent on proving his devotion to his feisty Vilna-born wife who had, as he would write, "seduced" him "into enterprises from which I might have remained apart without her." Among these, he named his "emergence as a propagandist for the Jews of Europe and Palestine." (She later referred to "'our' propaganda," and made clear her own passionate commitment to their people's struggle, though for such an independent spirit, she described her role in coy and not entirely convincing terms, calling herself "the Betsy Ross type of female who loves to sew flags for the men who are doing something interesting.") Elsewhere Hecht would chalk up his actions during these years to the tug of an older familial bond— all the tantes and uncles with whom he'd sung in Yiddish and munched pickles on those magical summer evenings in Racine. "It was they," he claimed, "who were under attack by the German murderers and the sly British. It was they who, long dead, suddenly set up a cry in me for Palestine." Sentimentality and scorn always mingled in Hecht, while his strong romantic streak tended to split humanity into powerful, sharkish villains and put-upon, little-fish heroes—those he felt deserved his venom and those he viewed as desperately needing his defense. As word trickled in of the horrors engulfing Europe, he knew in his gut who was who.

That said, there's something too pat about Hecht's account of this chronic attack of late-onset tribalism. All his tidy explanations for his sudden Jewish awakening don't really do justice to the far more contradictory and evolving blur of thoughts and emotions that appear to have propelled him in real time. In 1939, when, as he later wrote, "the German mass murder of the Jews . . . had recently brought my Jewishness to the surface," the German mass murder of the Jews hadn't yet begun. While the situation in Europe was clearly already dire, and

Hecht's eventual anger was absolutely actual, and visceral—"I saw the Germans as murderers with red hands," he would seethe, "their fat necks and round, boneless faces became the visages of beasts"—this was, it seems, a rage that built up over years and for multiple reasons, conscious and not. But that subtler, slower accretion of feeling had little room in Hecht's black-and-white retrospective recounting of how a fever had seized him in 1939.

In his letters from those very months, he sounds cheerful, engaged, and primarily concerned with things like bathing his dog, Googie, playing pinochle with Lederer, lifting barbells, negotiating a $5,500-a-week contract with "either Goldwyn, Selznick, or Metro," and helping "MacCheesecake" with a script rewrite. The screenplays poured out of him during this period and ranged terrifically—*Nothing Sacred, The Goldwyn Follies, Gunga Din, Wuthering Heights, It's a Wonderful World, Let Freedom Ring, Lady of the Tropics, Gone with the Wind, His Girl Friday, Comrade X* are among the nearly two dozen movies he wrote, cowrote, or rewrote between 1937 and 1940, when he also directed (without MacArthur) the most smoothly polished and even Hollywoody of his own films, a melancholy modern fairy tale, *Angels over Broadway*, starring Rita Hayworth and Douglas Fairbanks Jr.

And on the rare occasions when the looming European war surfaced in his correspondence, it was generally cast in offhand, almost breezily dismissive terms, as in a May 1940 telegram sent from Beverly Hills to Rose, in Nyack: "DARLING I AM BUSIER ... THAN A TRANSATLANTIC BROADCASTER THE WILD NEWS FROM HOLLAND AND ENGLAND MUSTNT SLOW YOU OR ME UP WARS WONT HELP US GET ANYWHERE BUT IN THE SOUP I MISS YOU BUT FEEL TOO PREOCCUPIED TO WORRY." He then went on about how they might consider renting a certain "BEACH HOUSE THATS A HONEY" and so on. Also evident was his usual mildly amused disgust with the way he felt he was frittering his days and his talents. In a letter from around the same time, he wrote

With Hayworth on set, *Angels over Broadway*

Gene Fowler that he'd been "playing parachute pete the life saver on all sorts of movies—stirring up the bilge with my fountain pen, adding drops of chlorine here and little lumps of quicklime there and Rescuing, as they call it, the Produce. I feel relaxed perhaps because all my notions about Hollywood— sort of cooked up on the run and never very deep in my blood stream—have flowered and my soul is lush with a tropic under-brush of loathing, contempt and righteousness in which I lurk like the last of the head hunters."

And yet . . . those early days with the circus people of Ra-cine had apparently left their mark, as Hecht had always been a master juggler—able to keep several scripts, women, ideas, ca-reers in the air at once. Now, more than ever, the same mental ambidexterity held. Even as he'd been tossing off and tuning up these multiple screenplays and writing for the stage, he had also begun an ambitious work of fiction that in peculiar ways predicted what was next for himself and, indeed, for the world.

When he first mentioned *A Book of Miracles* in a letter to Rose, he sounded almost sunny about it, describing it as "a curious project I've bounced into—it's something like the Bible. Tell my Pa I'm writing about Angels. He will understand . . ." A few letters later he declared that "the whole thing will be my Arabian Nights . . . lusty and unflagging and hilarious. . . . And when I am done with it, I am done with writing as I call writing. I will have sung my song and told the story of my mind and shown all the sides of my wit and whatever I do afterward will be for diversion." As he threw himself into composing this magnum opus, comprising a series of novellas and lengthy short stories, certain themes began to emerge: "I am," he gushed to Rose, "so full of Jewish history that I feel a yamulka growing on my head." The darkly comical tome that resulted was a decidedly mixed bag—sometimes inspired, often long-winded, now and then sparkling, frequently indulgent, and occasionally jarring in its abrupt lurches between the satirical and the saccharine, with blackly comic send-ups of Hollywood producers and radio advertising executives bumping uneasily against overwrought and apparently sincere kitsch allegories featuring saintly bearded holy men, learned rabbis, heavenly choirs. God himself even puts in a few cameos. As does the European carnage to come. And in this sense, the book stands as more than just another volume on the Ben Hecht bookshelf: it also seems a kind of prophecy—in which Hecht's hyperactive imagination finally met its real-world match.

Written in 1937 or 1938, edited closely by the book's dedicatee, Rose, and published in 1939—that fateful year—the first story in the collection, "The Little Candle," is a "fiction" that unfolds as a kind of nightmare premonition of the dreadful day sometime in the unspecified near future when "we Jews opened our morning newspapers . . . unprepared," he writes, "for what we were to read. . . . We stared with nausea and disbelief at the print. For . . . we found that the cloud we had watched so long and, in a way, so aloofly, had grown suddenly black and dreadful and immense. It filled all the pages of the journals. The world had made, it seemed, but a single face overnight and this face thrust itself into our breakfast hour, ugly and hellish. Like a monster evoked out of the smoking pages of our history, it confronted us, exultant and with the ancient howl of massacre on its lips."

"It" was what he dubbed in the story "the great International Pogrom"—the (still only imaginary when he was writing) slaughter overnight of half a million European Jews and the driving "from their homes and hunt[ing] into forests, deserts, and mountains" of another million. "On this July morning," Hecht spoke pointedly now in the first-person collective, without a trace of his usual detachment or scoffing, "we were Jews again, whatever our previous conceptions of ourselves had been; Jews, battered and crushed and exiled once more from the pretense of fellowship. Not only was there in us that common denominator that echoed the cries of agony and death, that sent our spirits cowering beside the myriads of unknown Jews in the shambles of Europe, but the eyes of our host, however compassionate, segregated us into sudden ghettoes of grief."

Ben Hecht had at last found a cause worthy of his formidable fury. His allegiance to that cause—and to that fury—would in many ways determine the course of the rest of his life.

Another less melodramatic but no less meaningful aspect of Hecht's character became, he maintained, more pronounced in and around this time: "Oddly," he wrote, "in addition to becoming a Jew in 1939 I became also an American—and remained one."

Just as he'd always been a Jew, Hecht had of course been an American since he first drew breath, but the need to reaffirm the fact of his citizenship—and to link it to his Jewishness—is telling, as he seemed determined to convince any skeptics that, whatever his outspoken commitment to the besieged Jews of Europe, to Palestine, and eventually to the state of Israel, America was and would forever be his home.

As it happened, most of Hecht's earliest gestures on behalf of the Jews emerged as part of a wider American war effort—and in far more soaring tones than the haunting minor keys that would later mark his explicitly Jewish work in this vein. When in July of 1940, Alfred Hitchcock was putting the finishing touches on *Foreign Correspondent*—set in Europe during the two weeks in 1939 before England declared war on Germany—producer Walter Wanger hired Hecht to pull an actual all-nighter and plot a late-breaking new ending for the film. In the movie's theatrical final moments, written by Hecht, Joel McCrea's New York crime reporter–turned–journalistic expert in Nazi espionage, Johnny Jones, a.k.a. Huntley Haverstock, stands before a microphone in a London radio station and begins his broadcast from a script: "Hello, America! I've been watching a part of the world being blown to pieces. A part of the world as nice as Vermont and Ohio and Virginia and California and Illinois lies ripped up and bleeding like a steer in a slaughter-house. And I've seen things that make the history of the savages read like Pollyanna legends—" But then the electricity cuts out, the bombs begin loudly to fall (this was still a kind of fiction, or prediction, and wouldn't happen in reality until five days after the scene was shot), and as "The Star-Spangled Banner" starts up, darkness descends, and Jones improvises a stirring plea: "Keep those lights burning! Cover them with steel, ring them with guns! Build a canopy of battleships and bombing planes around them. Hello, America! Hang on to your lights! They're the only lights left in the world!"

However inspiring, this monologue wasn't actually a direct call for the United States to take on Germany so much as it was an exhortation to remain alert, be prepared. (The Hollywood Production Code of the time prohibited such overt calls, and its enforcers had warned Wanger that the script ran the risk of "raising, and dramatizing . . . controversial racial and political questions . . . with the inevitable result of arousing audience feeling against the present German regime." Though adjustments were made to address these concerns, that most discriminating of film buffs, Joseph Goebbels, for one, considered the finished version of *Foreign Correspondent* "a masterpiece of propaganda.") Hecht's own position was much more explicitly interventionist, as he made plain when—under the auspices of the Fight for Freedom Committee, a nonpartisan organization that urged U.S. entry into the war well before Pearl Harbor and which was conceived in response to the isolationism of Charles Lindbergh's America First Committee—he and MacArthur joined forces to write a rousing patriotic revue with the incongruously, or maybe deliberately, silly title, *Fun to Be Free*, which was performed before seventeen thousand in Madison Square Garden on October 5, 1941. With music by Irving Berlin and Kurt Weill, the pageant opened as Bill "Bojangles" Robinson, in gold pants and ermine, tap-danced on top of a replica of Hitler's coffin and a gospel choir sang "When That Man Is Dead and Gone." Jack Benny, Helen Hayes, Ethel Merman, Betty Grable, George Jessel, and numerous other stars spoke earnestly and performed boisterously; New York Mayor Fiorello La Guardia, former Republican presidential candidate Wendell Willkie, and Brooklyn Dodgers manager Leo Durocher made speeches. ("We don't want Hitlerism, we want Americanism," declared Durocher, taking a break from the World Series then in progress. "And the Yankees are a great ball club. Even if we lose, we'll be losing in a free country.") Eddie Cantor wore a hoopskirt, Carmen Miranda sang, producer Billy Rose proclaimed that "the present war is between people who insist on laughing and people who can't laugh to save their souls from hell," and Hecht and MacArthur offered a playful, almost comic book meditation on what America is: "Some people think it's a piece of map shaped like a wisdom tooth and colored like a handful of lollypops. Some people think America is a dollar sign with a halo over it. Some people think the U.S.A. is an ostrich with a red, white and blue tail feather," and so on, through "the goldarndest collection of railroad ties, window panes, manhole covers, wheatfields, electric signs, apple pies and steel mills ever assembled within the boundaries of one nation." In fact, "the real show is inside them and behind them. We're here to tell you America is an idea: and the U.S.A. a dream. . . . Since the hour it was born and to the hour it dies—if it ever dies—it has been and will remain an idea, the simplest and yet most difficult idea ever hatched by the human mind—the idea of Freedom."

At the same time he and MacArthur were cooking up their punchy pageant script, Hecht had taken on a new—or, really, recycled—assignment, as Rose had arranged with Ralph Ingersoll, editor of the lively progressive tabloid *PM*, for him to resuscitate his "1,001 Afternoons" column there—though these afternoons would unfold in New York. Launched in 1940, Ingersoll's popular, photo-packed paper was devoted to a plenty Hechtian notion: "We are," proclaimed the enterprising editor, who'd helped make the fortunes of *Fortune*, *The New Yorker*, *Time*, and *Life*, "against people who push other people around." And starting in January 1941, Hecht would devote his daily essays in *PM* to variations on this theme, broadly construed—with sketches of various sympathetic Bowery bums, entrepreneurial tattoo artists, elderly grocers, and exquisitely dressed black doormen alternating with portraits of a familiar cast of characters: Bodenheim, Sherwood Anderson, Hecht's old friend the Polish sculptor Stanisław Szukalski all put in appearances. The point of view in the pieces "plays weathervane," as he described

With Rose

it, "to a great many winds," and while a fair number of the articles seem rather tired rehashes of those he'd written with more vigor when in Chicago, what *was* new was a pronounced, often pugilistic, approach to talking about Jews, about Nazis, about people who push Jews around.

And here he wasted no time in staking his ground, swinging a punch in one of his very first columns in the direction of former American ambassador to England and erstwhile movie studio head Joseph Kennedy, who had recently been holding meetings with "the important Jews of Hollywood and New York" and giving them "some *sub rosa* advice on what to do with their importance." These meetings have since been recounted elsewhere. (The most notorious of them took shape as a lunch thrown by the Warner brothers in late 1940, at which Kennedy held forth before the assembled for a full three hours.) But Hecht seems to have been the first to blurt their contents in such a public forum, announcing that "Joe has been giving advice to his Semitic Hollywood pals. He has been advising them to lie low, not to attract attention to themselves," since "anything the movies do to decry the horrors of Hitlerism will act as a boomerang and come back and knock over all the Jews." According to Hecht, when Kennedy had "concluded his missionary work, most of the screen rajahs were convinced that the best course open to Jews was to make themselves small, and walk gently as if they had a venereal disease. This would keep people from noticing them and calling them warmongers." The subject of Jews may or may not have been new to him, but the biting tone and nervy stance were classic Hecht, as was the object of his contempt—those who would tiptoe and lower their voices for fear of causing offense. And while the targets of some of his previous jabs (the unwitting parents of his first wife, for instance) might not have deserved it, this was something else. Given all that was happening in the world, Hecht's strong rhetorical right hook—aimed at a bullying isolationist and appeaser-of-Nazis like Joe Kennedy and the powerful yet suddenly cowering Jewish studio heads—seemed a wholly proportional response.

Hecht now wrote often and defiantly of Jews. He seemed to relish repeating that word, brandishing it, rubbing it in people's faces, maybe even trying to make his readers a little uncomfortable with it. Not surprisingly, his obsessive return to the theme got attention (that was the idea)—outrage and approval greeted his articles in the usual Hechtian proportions—and it was because of one of these columns that, as he'd eventually put it, "I bumped into history." Writing some ten years after the fact, Hecht remembered that the article that set this process in motion had been a particularly emphatic piece from April 1941, "My Tribe Is Called Israel," in which he pledged allegiance to a flagless people—"I write of Jews today, I who never knew himself as one before, because that part of me which is Jewish is under a violent and ape-like attack. My way of defending myself is to answer as a Jew . . ."—though the archival record makes it clear that the article that brought about Hecht's collision with history was in fact the more quietly enraged if no less potent "These Were Once Conquerors," published in August that year. In this article, he describes in detail a photo "allegedly taken by Gestapo agents 'just for fun'" and smuggled out of Poland—in which five laughing German aviators watch as their commanding officer, "solemnly and with a convulsing pretense of politeness," shaves the beard from a Jew they've "lassooed" in the streets of Warsaw. The officer is, Hecht wrote, pulling the whiskers from "his cornered Jew . . . as you might pluck . . . feathers from a dead chicken." The Jew, meanwhile, "stands looking directly into the averted eyes of his tormentor. And if this young Jew were standing on a rostrum in Jerusalem many years ago, receiving the acclaim of his people, his eyes could hold no prouder look."

The article prompted several notable communications—one from Groucho Marx, who effused, "I was so enrapt with your piece in PM that I frantically phoned you all over town, trying to snare you to dinner. It was wonderful! That's what we need—a little more belligerency, professor, and not quite so much cringing!" The other, more fateful response was a telegram from a stranger, one Peter H. Bergson, writing on behalf of something he called, a bit cryptically, the Jewish Army Committee to thank Hecht for having given in his latest article "magnificent expression to the pride and spiritual heroism which for centuries accumulated in the soul of the genuine and conscious Jew. By the creation of a Jewish army we intend to transform this heroic spirit into heroic deeds." It seems Hecht didn't reply, but after several weeks, Bergson tried again, and sent him a longer letter declaring in his forceful if slightly stilted English, "We are following with tenseness and admiration your proud and illuminating pronouncements on the problems concerning the plight and hopes of the Jewish people," and asking whether Hecht would consider giving his "illustrious name to the Jewish national cause, as you understand it." This second appeal registered, and Hecht agreed, if nothing else, to a drink at the 21 Club.

It was a most unlikely meeting of the minds. Here he was—a middle-aged, pork-chop-eating, Christmas-tree-lighting dyed-in-the-American-wool wise guy who "disliked causes . . . disliked public speaking . . . never attended meetings of any sort . . . had no interest in Palestine and had always bolted any conversation about a Jewish homeland." And there was Bergson, a dashing young Lithuanian-born Palestinian activist, passionately committed to the cause of national Jewish liberation as conceived by the intellectual and ideological firebrand Ze'ev Jabotinsky. Bergson's real name was Hillel Kook, but when he'd come to the United States in 1940, as an emissary of the Irgun Tzvai Leumi, the militant Palestinian underground, he had adopted an alias to avoid embarrassing his relatives, many of whom—his father, various cousins, and uncles—were well-known rabbis and Torah scholars. One of his father's brothers, Abraham Isaac Kook, was the first Ashkenazi chief rabbi of Palestine and among the leading Jewish spiritual figures of the day.

Although he'd been considered a religious prodigy as a boy, Bergson/Kook had chosen a different path, of radical politics and unabashed secularism. But charisma and a knack for leadership were apparently in his genes, and soon after he'd crossed the Atlantic, he assumed control of the small cadre of Irgunists

Peter Bergson

who had been sent to America to raise funds and popular support for a Jewish army, based in Palestine, to fight with the Allies against Hitler. (Less explicit in their official statements yet obvious to those in the know was their simultaneous desire to create military facts on the Middle Eastern ground, to protect locally against perceived Arab threats and, eventually, to free Palestine from the British.) While that larger force was still only theoretical, the U.S.-based Irgunists considered themselves, in the words of one of the men, "a unit of a liberation army." With Bergson acting as their commander, this disciplined group of self-declared soldiers became widely known as the Bergsonites, the Bergson Group, or—as if they were a nattily dressed, Near Eastern swing band—the Bergson Boys. With scant money and even less idea of the United States and its Jews, they immediately began organizing, trying by any means possible to win the support of influential Americans, Jews and non-Jews, partisans and nonpartisans alike.

This was of course all news to Hecht, who sipped his drink and listened as the brash, mustachioed twenty-six-year-old Bergson and one of his Palestinian comrades enthused in grand terms about his *PM* columns and told him about Jabotinsky. Hecht claimed he'd never heard of the recently deceased novelist, journalist, and founder of the hard-line nationalistic movement known as Revisionism. Buying them several rounds of drinks, "unaware that neither had eaten that day," Hecht explained that he had no interest in Palestine and that his main concern was the cowardice of those influential American Jews who took pains to avoid speaking out about what was happening to their kinsmen in Europe. As Hecht remembered it, "both men smiled politely at my irritation with their Palestine talk, and their sudden silence on the subject impressed me as something more than good manners." He was struck, too, by "a pride in them, as if these two stray 'fans' who had sought to meet me were somehow men of importance." Perhaps it was because of this pride, this perceived importance, that Hecht didn't just say goodbye then and there, but agreed to meet them again, at the Algonquin suite where he was staying while Rose was off on one of her Hollywood stints.

Bergson himself later confirmed the substance of this meeting, calling it "all true except the part where we were hungry— physically hungry. That was also true, but not on that day. You know, a writer fuses things."

Despite Hecht's protestations of indifference and unsuitability, Bergson wasn't easily dissuaded, and he had glimpsed an opening in the writer's willingness to meet again. Soon after that initial drink, the persistent Palestinian turned up at the Algonquin, accompanied by two of his deputies and a striking young woman in a black picture hat. According to Hecht's retrospective account, Bergson now announced that they wanted him to be the American leader of their campaign, and Hecht continued to insist they'd come knocking at the wrong door. "Their choice of me," he admitted, "made them seem naïve and a little overdesperate." The Middle East aside, politics in general were very far from Hecht. He had friends on all sides of the ideological wars that raged through Hollywood and New York during these years and considered himself not just unaffiliated but contentedly detached. "Your technique must be slipping," he had Eve Arden's tough-talking reporter character quip at Clark Gable in *Comrade X*, a ticklish *Ninotchka*-esque comedy written right around this time. "I've never known you to stoop to politics before."

But now his own technique threatened to slip—since, for all his reluctance to deal with Bergson and company, Hecht the shameless romantic was fascinated by the poise and slightly mysterious determination of his foreign visitors. Besides the hat-wearing Miriam Heyman—whom Hecht believed had been brought along that day as a pretty lure—Bergson was accompanied by the soft-spoken but broodingly fierce Kishinev-born, Sorbonne-educated journalist and former secretary to Jabotinsky, Samuel Merlin, and the native Tel Avivian, formerly left-wing agriculturalist now die-hard Revisionist political operative, Yitshaq "Mike" Ben-Ami. As Hecht talked with them, he grew, despite himself, more and more enchanted. Their eyes, he reported, flashed with "the mood of adventure." Their presence suggested some bold new way of being Jewish: "They were," he wrote, "unmarked by memories of suffering. The cries of dying Jews seemed not to echo out of their spirits. Instead they sat solemn with energies, like a group of knights dedicated to the rescue of a maiden in distress. The maiden was the Jew of Europe and the Jewish soul of the world." He went so far as to say that he looked on them as "perfect Jews."

This was, to be sure, yet another of his vivid reductions, since Bergson and his confederates were hardly perfect. They had, in fact, known Jewish suffering firsthand, and its memory seems to have been precisely what was driving them to act so assertively now. Hecht's vision of their cause as being a somehow Semitic variation on Camelot sounds more like cinematic wishful thinking than a reasoned perception based on the messy and often brutal political reality of 1940s Palestine. But his overheated fantasy did the trick. After wrangling a bit about the cumbersome title they'd chosen for themselves—The Committee for a Jewish Army of Stateless and Palestinian Jews ("unattractive," Hecht the crack rewrite man informed them, "and not very inspiring")—he urged them to make it absolutely clear that the army they were proposing wasn't intended for American Jews. He told them to keep their "hop-headed Palestinian nationalism" from creeping into their propaganda. And he agreed to help. Soon Hecht found himself cochairman of what he would come to refer to simply as "the Committee," even as its goals evolved dramatically and its name mutated multiple times over the ensuing years. His own objective throughout all those transmogrifications, he said, remained steady: "to help make a little more impressive the older and simpler title—Jew."

As Hecht was drawn to the Bergsonites, they were impressed by him. Bergson took an instant liking to the older man, and Mike Ben-Ami would write that as soon as they met him, they understood that his was "a voice that would catch America's ear, a voice from outside the Jewish establishment, uninhibited by political and parochial interests." He was, admittedly, "rough to tangle with. . . . He had a compassionate heart, covered up by a short temper, a brutal frankness and an acid tongue, [but] once he decided right from wrong on any issue, he mobilized all his faculties to fight for his beliefs with righteous fury." Ultimately he became, in Ben-Ami's estimation, the committee's "most important exponent in America."

Even as he continued with the usual whirl of his own work, Hecht got down to business on the Bergsonites' behalf—sending letters of introduction, contributing his own money to help cover their expenses (early on he gave them five thousand dollars, "an astronomical sum" at the time, according to Merlin)—and while he continued to question his fitness for this role, he pushed on. History had its own terrible momentum now, and he felt he had to act, both on the Jewish front and on a more general American battlefield. The day after Pearl Harbor, as the United States entered the war, Hecht—still juggling—published a bit of jingoistic doggerel in *PM*, "Uncle Sam Stands Up" ("The great big gabble-headed / Red white and blue galoot / Has drawn his Forty-four / And started in to shoot . . ."), and wrote Rose about casting his new play, his latest round of "Selznicking," and the general atmosphere: "The war swings like a huge aurora over the town and the dumb sense of security in which even American burglars & rapists go about clothed is being torn hourly from the streets. Generally the mood seems to be of someone who has been finally invited to a heady social function he was pretending to disdain."

That same month, the Committee officially established itself, and by early January 1942, it had managed to scrape together enough money from donations to take out a nearly full-page ad in the *New York Times*. Written by another Bergsonite literary recruit, the Christian Zionist journalist Pierre van Paassen, it blared, "JEWS FIGHT FOR THE RIGHT TO FIGHT" and announced that the Jews, "the first victims of Hitler's hatred and aggression, . . . are eager to fight back and to avenge." The ad did run in the *Times*—signed by a long list of congressmen, rabbis, bishops, and well-known cultural figures, from Reinhold Niebuhr to Ernst Lubitsch, Arnold Schoenberg, Paul Tillich, Melvyn Douglas, and Max Lerner—though its aristocratic Jewish publisher, Arthur Sulzberger, was reportedly distressed at the appearance in his own newspaper of the word JEW in big black capital letters. In general, the *Times* preferred to discreetly tuck small articles or ads about "Jewish matters" on the obituary page. (In his memoir of this period, Samuel Merlin speculates cogently that there were psychological reasons for this placement, revealing the publisher's sense, conscious or not, "that the Jews were doomed; that the most characteristic news about Jews is that they were dying.")

Such squeamishness at the boldface mention of the word JEW was something the Committee encountered often. When in early 1942 Rose and Miriam Heyman organized a mass meeting in Hollywood to raise money for the Jewish army campaign, they planned to send out hundreds of invitations in Hecht's name. Thinking this appeal would be more effective if several sponsors were listed, Rose convinced Lubitsch to sign, while Hecht tried to persuade the various Jewish studio heads to add their endorsements, and repeatedly ran into the same brick wall. All the moguls were ready to write checks on the sly to help Jewish causes, but they wanted nothing to do with outward displays of identification or support.

Rose, for her part, took these refusals as a goad. Not for nothing would Hecht later describe in somewhat fanciful terms the righteous troublemaker his wife had purportedly been as a child: "Time and again, overcome by some piece of sordidness or injustice, she would arise, usually on top of her desk, and denounce the teacher in three foreign languages. After that, the family would move to another neighborhood." Her commitment to the Bergsonites seemed only to intensify as others recoiled—and it appears her amped-up feelings affected Hecht, who redoubled his own efforts in turn. While she was on the West Coast that winter, putting the final touches on what would be her only credited Hollywood script, *Fingers at the Window,* a rather stiff and scattered psychological thriller about a serial ax murderer on the loose in Chicago, directed for MGM by Hecht's old friend and collaborator Charlie Lederer, Rose had thrown herself into work for the Committee, about which she seemed to feel a good deal more passion than she did for her day job. (Her letters from this time are filled with vague but pointed references to "those cheap Metro intrigues and cheaper betrayals" and "all that tormenting nastiness at Metro.") She was especially stirred by what she saw as the Bergsonites' old-world grit and ardor—as, for instance, when she wired Hecht from Los Angeles a few weeks before the mass meeting to describe an evening with the Mankiewiczes, the Lithuanian-born painter Max Band and his wife, and "THE JEWISH ARMY GIRLS WE SANG YIDDISH HEBREW AND RUSSIAN SONGS AND I MISSED YOU I ADORE YOU." In early January she telegraphed him to say that, for reasons unspecified, "TODAY LUBITSCH TURNED GER-MAN AGAIN AND WALKED OUT ON JEWISH ARMY." Meanwhile she "PHONED SELZNICK AND CALLED ON HIM TO RISE UP LIKE SAM-SON AGONISTES." Hecht thought his good friend might be more amenable to lending his name than the other bosses, but Selz-nick rebuffed him, explaining that he had no interest in what he deemed a Jewish political cause, because, as Hecht said Selz-nick said, "I'm an American and not a Jew." At which they made a deal. Hecht would ask three people of Selznick's choosing if they considered him an American or a Jew. If any one of them said "American," Selznick was off the hook. All three, though, said "Jew," with Leland Hayward even erupting, "For God's sake, what's the matter with David? He's a Jew and he knows it."

So it was that the reluctant producer signed his name along-side Hecht's, and one balmy evening a few months after Amer-ica entered the war, a sizable crowd filled the bunting-festooned Twentieth Century–Fox commissary. Charlie Chaplin, Harry Warner, Sam Spiegel, and various other illustrious film folk were on hand to hear speeches by Hecht, Bergson, Florida senator Claude Pepper, Burgess Meredith, and Colonel John Patterson —a freethinking Anglo-Irish officer and lion hunter who had, during the First World War, created with Jabotinsky what was known as the Jewish Legion, prototype of the Palestinian force that Bergson hoped to establish now. In Hecht's retelling of the evening's proceedings, Patterson was first greeted with cheers—as a strapping veteran of the British army, America's greatest ally against Hitler—but when he began to slam his own country for what he called its anti-Semitism and its discriminatory policies toward the Jews of Palestine, the mood in the room changed abruptly. Several people stormed out, some seemed merely bored by "the tale of British skullduggery in a distant desert," while others (gossip columnist Hedda Hopper first among them) grew excited and began pulling out their checkbooks, or promising to do so. By the end of the evening, $130,000 had been pledged to the Jewish army—though ultimately the Committee managed to collect only nine thousand of those dollars. "Thus," pronounced Hecht, "our first Jewish propaganda meeting was a fine success—if you care to overlook its failure."

Meanwhile, the gathering had apparently agitated Selznick, who had (as was his controlling wont) various ideas about how the Committee might more effectively present itself. Hecht sought to smooth his ruffled feathers in a letter: "Having sort of half hornswoggled you into the Cause I feel that any discomforts you've acquired out of our playing Jerusalem for an evening are my fault and I would like to minimize them in your eyes as they are in mine . . ." For all Hecht's public grandstanding, the letter offers a surprisingly sober off-the-record glimpse at his real-time thinking about this particular Cause and his own reasons for taking it up.

"I feel," he wrote, "that most of your alarms are those peculiar to the master showman who would like his product to be loved by all. Dear David, the Jewish Cause, however you serve and garnish, is not this kind of a product." Selznick was unsettled, it seems, about a possibly "unfavorable Gentile reaction," which Hecht dismissed as par for the course and/or beside the point. At the same time, "I know that most of our American friends of Jewish descent were highly stirred and much elated by our project. I know also that there were many who shook from head to toe and are still shaking. . . . I don't have to tell you that the only cause such Jews want to hear about are causes which will conceal from them and from the world any hint of their Jewishness. And the only thing you could sell such Jews is a magic wand to make them disappear—or a Moses named Throckmorton to come and take back the Ten Commandments, the Talmud, and the Star of David and put them back in that Bonfire out of which they originally came."

But Hecht had, he made clear, other ideas, which had driven him to join the Jewish army campaign. "I felt that the Jews have been trying to arouse all kinds of emotions in the world—pity, compassion, horror, guilt—and that it would do all of us a lot of good if they could, for a change, inspire some other kind of emotions, such as a home run or a successful battle inspires in the Americano. I felt that Jews like ourselves who are a little stronger than most owed it to throw not only a few dimes to the dolor of the Jew but to give him a lift with our strength, to add our voices to his battle cry rather than his moans."

No doubt he meant this thoughtful pep talk wholeheartedly. Though it was, of course, much easier to write such a sanguine thing in early 1942 than it would be even just a few months later, when the almost deafening sound of Jewish moaning would compel Ben Hecht to change his tack yet again.

8

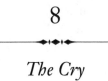

The Cry

ON "THE MOST TRAUMATIC DAY" of Peter Bergson's life (the words are his), November 25, 1942, a brief Associated Press story appeared on page 6 of the *Washington Post* and almost vanished beside boldfaced ads for Kessler's Blended Whiskey—"SMOOTH AS SILK but not High Hat"—and the U.S. Army—"MEN OF 18 and 19 *ENLIST TODAY* IN THE COAST ARTILLERY!" The headline was tiny, its implications enormous: "*2 Million Jews Slain, Rabbi Wise Asserts.*" According to the short article that followed, Stephen Wise, chairman of multiple major American Jewish organizations, had "learned through sources confirmed by the State Department" that approximately half the Jews of Nazi-occupied Europe had been killed in an "extermination campaign." According to these sources, Hitler had ordered the rest of the area's Jews wiped out by year's end.

Cataclysmic as this article was, its contents were both news and not news, as for months, unofficial word of the carnage had been dribbling out of Europe. As early as June 1942, a detailed report describing the murder of some 700,000 Eastern European Jews had been smuggled from Poland and broadcast on the BBC; during July, Yiddish papers in New York published accounts of massacres of Jews in the Soviet Union; and by August the State Department had received word from a reliable source of Hitler's plan to annihilate all the Jews of Nazi-controlled Europe. Wise also learned of the Final Solution that month, though he had agreed to withhold the improbable-sounding information from the public until the government could confirm it. That happened very slowly. The patrician functionaries at the State Department deemed this a relatively low priority in the midst of the war and were, it seems, skeptical of the veracity of the reports—both because they suggested false atrocity stories from the previous world war and because they came from "interested parties," that is, Jews. And when Wise finally received permission to speak, that tucked-away and almost telegraphic story (less than 120 words long) was the only immediate mention of the matter in the U.S. capital's paper of record. Several regional dailies ran reports of the rabbi's announcement on their front pages, but for the most part, this should-be earth-shattering news was relegated to a few paragraphs at the back of most American papers, near the want ads. Sulzberger's *New York Times* published a brief item on page 10—this one, too, oddly dwarfed by an enormous advertisement for whiskey.

Over breakfast in Washington that dark November day, Bergson read the *Post* article and began to tremble. (Hecht's "The Little Candle" had eerily predicted this very scene of shocked encounter with a morning newspaper and its report of mass Jewish slaughter.) The well-informed Palestinian activist had of course heard those other horror stories, but this was different—a credible account of a *systematic* program to eliminate Europe's Jews. Disbelieving, he ran to the State Department to question one of his contacts there, assistant secretary of state

Adolf Berle, who confirmed his worst fears, then asked with a shrug, "What can we do?" Winning the war would be, Berle and others around him argued, the best way to help the Jews. Bergson, however, knew that he and his committee couldn't just wait politely for Allied victory. By evening, he was back in New York, where the group had converged and begun to plot a new and much more aggressive campaign. Although they would continue their push for a Jewish army for some time, they also shifted gears and eventually renamed themselves nothing less than the Emergency Committee to Save the Jewish People of Europe.

Politicking was Bergson's passion, and since arriving in the United States he had devoted himself to lobbying for the cause. He had already won the support of various senators and representatives who'd issued proclamations endorsing the Jewish army idea and even introduced a resolution in Congress, calling for the same. ("How Peter loved resolutions!" Hecht wrote later, a little sardonically.) Hecht, meanwhile, had no such ambitions. His relationship with Bergson had been strained since that evening at the Fox commissary—after which Bergson made known his disappointment that Hecht hadn't instantly managed to raise several million dollars through his Hollywood connections. Hecht called Bergson's expectations "childish," and in an attempt to patch things up a few months later, Bergson wrote him of the "sad, somewhat tragic misunderstandings which were created between us during my California visit." But with Wise's announcement, they both seem to have realized that their little spat was beside the point. In the interest of Saving the Jewish People of Europe, they would put aside their differences and get to work.

Hecht's own impulse was to yank his pen from its holster and come out firing—which prompted him, that December, to dash off the scathing "Ballad of the Doomed Jews of Europe," to be published as a large, paid notice in the *New York Times*. (The Committee had already absorbed the lessons of those whiskey ads, which so dominated the pages on which they appeared. As one of the other Bergsonites, Eri Jabotinsky, son of Ze'ev, put it, they had realized the power of promoting their cause "just as you would advertise Chevrolet motor cars or Players cigarettes.") In big boxy letters, Hecht's poem blasted: "FOUR MILLION JEWS waiting for death / Oh hang and burn but—quiet, Jews! / Don't be bothersome; save your breath—/ The world is busy with other news." For several quatrains he ratcheted up the rhymes of "smear" and "here," "time" and "crime" as he built to his withering final stanza, and Hitler's promise to complete the extermination by the end of the year: "Oh World be patient—it will take / Some time before the murder crews / Are done. By Christmas you can make / Your Peace on Earth without the Jews."

Even for the quick-witted and decisive Bergson, Hecht may have been moving a little too fast. Between the time the ad was typeset and the newspaper printed, a copy somehow reached both the American Jewish Congress and the American Jewish Committee, whose officials were alarmed, since they feared that its publication might be perceived as "attacking Christmas." These biting lines of Hecht's would, they warned, save no Jews and, worse still, might backfire horribly—maybe even cause pogroms. Faced with vocal dismay on the part of these organizations—and one gray-haired Jewish judge who broke down weeping in his presence—Bergson agreed to withhold the ad, though when he told Hecht he'd done so, according to Bergson, "he nearly blew his top."

The ad appeared in the *Times* the next September, and no pogroms ensued. More astounding, "life," as Bergson put it, still reeling years later, "went on." Most Americans seemed oblivious to or unconcerned by the news of the catastrophe unfolding in Europe, and the Jewish leadership appeared paralyzed—all of which prompted Hecht to shift tonal gears and replace the bile of the ad with a beseeching appeal to the widest possible audience. "*Remember Us!*" implored the title of the article he published in the *American Mercury* in February 1943. One of the very first reports of the Holocaust-in-progress to surface in a mass-circulation American magazine, an abridged version appeared in *Reader's Digest* the same month, and it seemed designed to stoke not so much outrage as appalled compassion and, he hoped, action: "When the time comes to make peace," it begins, ". . . all the victims of the German adventure will be there to pass sentence—all but one: the Jew." The only words the murdered would be able to offer at that late date would be, Hecht warned, "the faint, sad phrase, *'Remember us!'*" The article then unleashed a grisly sort of incantation, spoken in the collective voice of the slaughtered, in whose name Hecht intoned, "*Remember us!* In the town of Freiburg in the Black Forest, two hundred of us were hanged and left dangling out of our kitchen windows to watch our synagogue burn and our rabbi flogged to death. . . . In Warsaw in the year 1941 we kept count and at the end of the 12 months 72,279 of us had died. Most of us were shot but there were thousands of us who were whipped and bayoneted to death . . ." And so on and on, through a not especially artful, though factually wrenching and passionately presented litany of far-flung towns and tortures, from Włocławek to the Ukraine, burning basements to bloodied rivers, each terrible tableau punctuated by that refrain from beyond the grave "*Remember us!*" Not only was this hardly standard *Reader's Digest* fare, such pathos-thick pleading was a sincere departure for Ben Hecht.

But by now he seemed willing to try any strategy for the sake of the cause. (He'd stopped insisting that he wasn't a man of causes.) At around the same time these articles came out, he arranged for a gathering of several dozen well-known literary and cultural figures at the Manhattan apartment of his friends the playwright and director George S. Kaufman and his witty editor wife, Bea. Each of the guests had successful novels or plays, poetry collections or musical scores to his or her name, and all of them were Jewish. "What would happen," Hecht wondered, "if these brilliant Jews cried out with passion against the German butchers? If these socially and artistically celebrated Jews spoke up in rage at the murder of their people! How they could dramatize the German crime! How loudly they could present the nightmare to America and the world!"

After he stood to speak—rattling off a list of gruesome facts and startling figures, and questioning the complacency of "England's great humanitarian, Churchill" as well as "our great keeper of the rights of man—Roosevelt" and "that third champion of all underdogs—Stalin"—there was silence. Whatever the urbane crew sipping coffee in the Kaufmans' living room that evening may have thought of Churchill or Stalin, even to imply criticism of Roosevelt in such a context was almost unheard of. Within a few minutes, half a dozen of the guests had marched out, as a livid Edna Ferber demanded to know: "Who is paying you to do this wretched propaganda? . . . Mister Hitler? Or is it Mister Goebbels?"

This is, it should be said, Ben Hecht's own account of what transpired that evening—which by now has a familiar ring. Like the Hollywood commissary gathering, this one ended, he said, with "anger and irritation" directed mostly toward *him* instead of the seemingly indifferent American, British, and Soviet governments or, for that matter, Mister Hitler and Mister Goebbels. In his telling, as Bea Kaufman walked him to the door, she apologized by explaining, "You asked them to throw away the most valuable thing they own—the fact that they are Americans," and Hecht, as usual, mused to himself that in fact her "highfalutin guests . . . had not behaved like Americans but like scared Jews[.] And what in God's name were they frightened of? Of people realizing they were Jews? But people knew that already."

While there's a regrettable tinge of self-righteous bluster at work in Hecht's depiction of his own as the sole brave voice in the wilderness, he was also quick to admit that during this period, "I was never less alone in my life." Never mind the tight knot of Bergsonites that now often surrounded him. That same evening at the Kaufmans' he'd won offers of help from two important artistic allies—director and playwright Moss Hart and composer Kurt Weill. They would soon band together with "a third Jew," as Hecht called him, theatrical impresario Billy Rose, and the four would get down to the business—really, the show business—of proving they weren't afraid.

That February was a busy month. First came an announcement by Hecht and Billy Rose of "a memorial service for the 2,000,000 European Jews massacred by the Nazis," to be performed at Madison Square Garden in March. "Religious in character and based upon Mr. Hecht's story 'Remember Us,'" according to an article in the *New York Times*, the production would be staged by "a large group of writers, artists and musicians . . . and will end with a mass prayer for the dead recited and sung by a choir of 500 voices." Billy Rose would produce and Hecht write, while Hart and Weill would direct and compose the music, respectively; they agreed it best to do this independently of the Bergsonites, to avoid what Hart characterized as getting "tie[d] up with any partisan Palestinian group." Better yet, they'd ask all the Jewish organizations in New York to cosponsor the spectacle.

Or try to. In his memoirs Hecht describes a Keystone Kops–like gathering in his Algonquin suite at which representatives of thirty-two American Jewish organizations were visibly moved as he read aloud excerpts from his script-in-progress and Weill played his score on the piano. But when, on behalf of their "small Broadway propaganda group," Hecht asked the assembled to work together, by merely placing their organizations' names on the same letterhead and endorsing the production as one, the event devolved rapidly into "a free-for-all, bitter as a Kentucky feud," in which nearly everyone present wound up, in Hecht's possibly only slightly exaggerated recounting, "denouncing each other as Socialists, as Fascists, as Christians, as undesirables of every stripe." In the end, Hecht and his artistic collaborators were left in a room strewn with crumpled Yiddish newspapers and forgotten umbrellas, empty of everyone except Merlin, Ben-Ami, and Bergson, who shook his head and explained wearily, "Jews must always battle Jews. It's the only politics open to a stateless people. The only victories they can hope to enjoy are victories over each other."

He was soon proven more than right. Within days—while casting for the memorial pageant got under way and Hecht continued to work on his script ("immers[ing] himself in research," according to Ben-Ami, "delving into Jewish history and lore with a vengeance, as if to punish himself for all the years during which he had ignored his heritage")—the Bergsonites found themselves facing the fiercest opposition they'd encountered so far, all of which came from fellow Jews. Whether or not they saw this coming—or even (in Hecht's case) courted it—is debatable, but the response to their doings this month would have long-term implications, for better and worse, for their ability to alter American attitudes and policies toward the suffering Jews of Europe.

On February 13, 1943, a small item appeared in the *New York Times*, reporting that the Rumanian government had approached officials of the still-unchartered United Nations and offered to transfer to "any refuge selected by the Allies" the seventy thousand Jews who remained in the occupied area of Transnistria. The Rumanians had themselves already killed tens of thousands of Jews, but the *Times* article cited various "observers" who viewed this proposal as evidence that the government of fascist prime minister Ion Antonescu was "no longer confident of an Axis victory." In exchange for the surviving Jews' release, the Rumanians would levy a fee per refugee, to cover the cost of travel expenses. The U.N. had, according to the article, so far made no decision on the matter.

With Billy Rose and Bergson

But Hecht and the Bergsonites certainly had. And whatever
the blurriness surrounding the authorship of various Hollywood scripts on which Hecht may have worked over the years,
the identity of the writer responsible for the huge *Times* ad that
appeared just three days later could not have been more obvious. Not only did Hecht compose it in what Merlin called "one
inspired stroke," he signed it personally, and breathed into it all
his most corrosive rage and wit:

FOR SALE to Humanity
70,000 Jews
Guaranteed Human Beings at $50 a Piece

"Roumania is tired of killing Jews," it, or he, went on. "It has killed one hundred thousand of them in two years"—an exaggeration, though not a gross one. "Roumania will now give Jews away practically for nothing." The article detailing the offer appeared on one side of the ad, while a note on Committee letterhead was affixed above, addressed to the FOUR FREEDOMS—the "essential human freedoms" (of speech, of worship, from want, from fear) that Roosevelt had famously outlined in his 1941 state of the union address—care of the U.N. leaders:

> My Dear Noble State of Mind:
>   I know you are very busy, too busy perhaps to read the story on the left hand side of this page.
>   For that reason I am writing an ad. Ads are easier and quicker to read than stories.
>   Your admirer,
>   Ben Hecht

The usual clippable Committee coupon appeared below, asking that checks be sent to the Fifth Avenue address of their national headquarters and that donors lend their support to the campaign "to save European Jewry by action—not pity."

The ad had been intended, in Hecht's words, "to shock Jews, infuriate Jews and set them to screaming." Unfortunately, he wrote, "This they did, chiefly at me. I was, said the Jewish country clubs, the Zionists, the other Jewish organizations, a liar and a sensation monger, trying to attract attention to myself—and nothing more. I had dragged the name Jew down to a new low." While it's sometimes difficult to verify Hecht's claims about the outrage he bragged that he'd stirred in one scandalous context or another, in this case, it's easy enough. The response was swift, loud and, indeed, pitiless, with the most prominent figure of establishment American Judaism, that same Rabbi Stephen Wise, leading the charge. This reform rabbi and liberal Zionist leader—once powerful and principled, now rather sickly though still power-conscious and chronically decorous (or, to hear Hecht and the other Bergsonites tell it, insufferably pompous)—immediately began issuing indignant statements and writing agitated letters condemning the Committee and calling the ad "a hoax on the part of the Ben Hecht group." Wise had held unchallenged sway for several decades over the organized American Jewish community, on whom the pitch-black irony of Hecht's ad appeared utterly lost; it was denounced as "abominable" by various Zionist newspapers, the Committee accused of trying to "sell" Jews. Decades later, one of Wise's more hagiography-prone biographers would still bristle when describing this "extremist group [that] wanted nothing more than to call attention to its members as Jews, and of an especially militant variety. . . . Bergson and Hecht, under no discipline, could issue the most outrageous statements, well aware that they would face no reprisals."

In a way, though, Hecht the Hollywood gadfly and only recently self-aware Jew was an easier target for Wise than Bergson, who would in the end prove the real object of the rabbi's bizarrely engorged animus. With time, the aging and ailing Wise's hostility to the dynamic young Palestinian would swell into something of a vendetta, "personal, ideological and generational," in the words of another of the rabbi's biographers, who also has the decency to describe Wise's reaction to Bergson as "shameful." At a moment in history when his energies would best have been spent applying severe pressure on the Roosevelt administration—and doing anything else humanly possible to rally the world to save Europe's Jews—he instead moved heaven and earth to try and discredit Peter Bergson, whom he declared, in all seriousness, "as great an enemy of the Jews as Hitler." Ostensibly critical of the radical Jabotinskyite politics dear to Bergson and his group—"revisionist fascists," he called them (he was hardly alone in this estimation)—and adamant that the committee was no more than a ragtag gang of interlopers, with no mandate to speak on behalf of American Jewry, Wise also insisted that their noisy methods would provoke anti-Semitism in the United States. While these concerns may have been genuine, so was the fact that even the rabbi's admirers considered him an extreme egotist who couldn't bear to share the stage with anyone else; he clearly felt a profound threat to his own authority. If anything, it was Bergson's very knack for winning popular support that made him such a menace.

Because whatever insults Wise and his representatives hurled at them, Bergson and Hecht had already won the battle for public opinion, and in the wake of the "For Sale" ad's publication, donations poured into the Committee's offices. Some of those sending checks seem to have believed their money was going directly to fund the rescue of Rumania's Jews, which was not the case. (In fact, no one ever stepped forward to save them, as the State Department shrugged off the Rumanian overtures as "without foundation," the work of "the German propaganda machine." Public dismissals aside, however, there is ample evidence that the offer was legitimate and that the Allied governments were simply reluctant to take in so many refugees. The British Foreign Office announced itself "concerned with the difficulty of disposing of any considerable number of Jews," while one high-ranking American diplomat summed up the U.S. position with the chilling pronouncement that intervening on behalf of Rumania's Jews would "open the question of similar treatment for Jews in Hungary. . . . So far as I know we are not ready to tackle the whole Jewish problem.") With the money raised from the ad, the Committee was able to publish another ad the next week in papers across the country. Signed by Colorado senator Edwin C. Johnson and thirty-three other senators, thirteen governors, multiple ambassadors, and military men, along with Hecht and Arturo Toscanini, "THE PEOPLE HAVE SPOKEN," it proclaimed, *"But Their Officials Are Still Mute!"* The tremendous response to the first ad—according to the sec-

ond ad, whose tone and slightly awkward prose point to Bergson or Merlin, not Hecht, as author—"revealed that the American people are a part of Humanity first and not of Tweedledum
Politics." The follow-up ad also announced that on March 9
the "mass memorial," now titled *We Will Never Die*, would take
place at Madison Square Garden. A week before that date, the
New York Herald Tribune ran an editorial under the headline
"They Will Never Die," which described the upcoming pageant
as "the definitive answer to 'Mein Kampf' " and quoted Hecht's
script: "Let them who die helplessly make stronger the arm of
all those who fight."

News of the memorial-in-progress had attracted a great
deal of attention since it was first announced—and all the an-
ticipation seems to have further agitated Wise, who had, according to Hecht, telephoned him at the Algonquin. In "sonorous and impressive" tones that Hecht admitted irritated him
("I had never known a man with [such] a . . . voice who wasn't
either a con man or a bad actor") Wise announced that he'd
read the script, disapproved, and wanted Hecht both to cancel
the performance and to cease and desist his activities on behalf
of the Jews. "If you wish hereafter to work for the Jewish Cause,
you will please consult me and let me advise you." At this,
Hecht claimed he hung up—a possibly apocryphal twist, but a
nice symbolic summary of his attitude toward Wise and all the
stuffed-shirt, short-sighted bombast Hecht felt he embodied.
Sometime after this conversation the rabbi had actually gone
so far as to arrange for his alphabet soup of organizations to
schedule their own Madison Square Garden program—"in view
of the information that the Jewish Army Committee is planning a similar meeting"—to be held just a week before the Committee's pageant. Offers by the Bergsonites to join forces and
make the events into one were, in Merlin's words, "hooted
down." At the same time, Wise had lobbied New York governor
Thomas Dewey to cancel the official statewide day of mourning

he'd agreed to declare, to coincide with the performance of *We Will Never Die*. Denouncing the Bergsonites as "dangerous and irresponsible racketeers," Wise warned the governor of "the terrible disgrace" they were bringing "on our already harassed people." The governor chose to proceed with the day of mourning, which no doubt only further enraged Wise, as he and his deputies put the final touches on their own Madison Square Garden event.

A political rally of a certain stately, old-fashioned sort, Wise's gathering drew some twenty thousand people and featured speeches by the rabbi himself, Zionist leader Chaim Weizmann, Mayor La Guardia, several labor leaders, and a bishop, while "messages of sympathy and support" were offered in absentia by the archbishop of Canterbury, the chief rabbi of England, Governor Dewey, and other dignitaries. An eleven-point resolution was proposed, for submission to Roosevelt and the United Nations; a rabbi blew a ram's horn; a cantor sang the traditional Jewish funeral prayer for the ascent of the soul, a second rabbi recited the Mourner's Kaddish, a third read a psalm.

But no matter how dignified or heartfelt, this solemn, restrained, and entirely predictable program couldn't hold a theatrical candle to the flamboyantly spectacular Hecht-Hart-Rose-Weill production—a kind of Jewish passion play, featuring a nearly literal cast of thousands and performed twice on the night of March 9, 1943, before the largest crowd that had ever assembled at the Garden, forty thousand people, along with a throng that gathered outside to listen to the live radio broadcast on loudspeakers. In an auditorium swathed in twenty-five hundred yards of draped black cloth, on a stage dominated by two towering tablets inscribed with the ten commandments, Paul Muni, Edward G. Robinson, Sylvia Sydney, Luther Adler, star of the Yiddish theater Jacob Ben-Ami, and tenor Kurt Baum of the Metropolitan Opera all appeared, along with hundreds

We Will Never Die

of cantors, dozens of rabbis, scores of children from a New York Jewish orphanage, and the NBC symphony orchestra.

Somber, pious, elaborate in its austerity, and almost bullying in its high-minded mawkishness, this was a far cry from the tap-dancing, wisecracking realm of *Fun to Be Free* and its all-American antics. Hecht himself had described his goal with *We Will Never Die* as being "to bring a Madison Square Garden audience to the large grave of Jewry and let them stand for two hours looking into its remarkable contents." And the very massive scale of the production seemed almost to be its point. The Jews had, in Hecht's terms, suffered more and achieved more than any people throughout history—the triumphalism went both ways—and the pageant was meant to dramatize these extremes by means of its extravagant proportions.

As Weill's score fused strains of the Zionist anthem "Hatikva," with "Kol Nidre," the most haunting melody of the Day of Atonement, Hecht's script veered from incantation to prayer to a potted history lesson ("Long ago there was a tribe that tended sheep and tilled the ground in the half barren places beyond the Jordan River . . .") The action then shifted to an almost absurdly over-inclusive "roll call" of Jewish prophets and heroes, reaching from Moses, King David, Rashi, and Spinoza to Siegfried Marcus, "inventor of the benzone-propelled engine," and John Howard Payne, "American dramatist and author of the song 'Home Sweet Home,'" through Herzl and Freud, Samuel Gompers and Emin Pasha. After a rousing tribute to Jewish soldiers and fighters across the ages—Bar Kochba, Joseph Trumpeldor, Barney Ross—the pageant proceeded to its most relentlessly lugubrious section, based on Hecht's *American Mercury* and *Reader's Digest* articles, in which pale-faced, kerchiefed, and skullcapped actors, meant to be the murdered Jews of Europe's cities and shtetls, recounted in mournful monotone the atrocities perpetrated against them by the Germans, each monologue punctuated with the words *"Remember us!"* Not just a martyrology but also a call to arms, this sequence mounted to a proclamation of "the message from the dead—avenge us." As narrators Muni and Robinson took turns declaiming: this was not a Jewish problem. It was a "problem that belongs to humanity. . . . The corpse of a people lies on the steps of civilization. Behold it. Here it is! And no voice is heard to cry halt to the slaughter, no government speaks to bid the murder of human millions end." But "we here tonight have a voice. Let us raise it . . ." and so on, into the soaring strains of that choir of a hundred cantors in white robes, chanting the Mourner's Kaddish.

Over the course of the next four months, at least 100,000

people saw productions of the pageant, funded and promoted across the country by local committees. For the mid-April performance in Washington, D.C.—which took place just a week before the so-called Bermuda Conference, where the "refugee problem" was to be euphemistically discussed by American and English officials, sequestered at a pointed physical remove from any and all who might protest governmental inaction when it came to the rescue of the Jews—Hecht revised the script, to address directly the powerful conclave assembled by invitation only in Constitution Hall. "We the actors who have performed for you tonight are nearly done," explained one of the narrators, in the Prospero-like closing address. "But there is another cast of actors involved in this tale whose performance is not done. This cast is our audience . . ." At this, the seven Supreme Court justices present, as well as the thirty-eight senators, two hundred eighteen congressmen, dozens of ambassadors, attachés, cabinet secretaries, assistant secretaries, chiefs, deputies, commissioners, and Eleanor Roosevelt herself must have sat up a little straighter in their seats. "As much by the silence of the world as by the howl of the posse has the Jew been condemned. The silence of our history makers has made them honorary members of the German posse."

However brazen that accusation, the first lady seemed not to have taken offense, as in her nationally syndicated "My Day" column published soon after, she called *We Will Never Die* "one of the most impressive and moving pageants I have ever seen. No one who heard each group come forward and give the story of what had happened to it at the hands of a ruthless German military will ever forget those haunting words, 'Remember us.'" Though Mrs. Roosevelt studiously avoided mentioning the Jews as victims of that ruthlessness—as would the delegates of the Bermuda Conference—the memorial's message finally seemed to be seeping out to reach a more general American audience. As they took it on the road, Hecht and his collaborators con-

tinued to adjust the pageant to keep up with the major historical events then unfolding—the Warsaw Ghetto uprising, most
notably—and other actors and supporters signed on. In Philadelphia Claude Rains joined the cast, in Boston, Ralph Bellamy,
and in Chicago, Burgess Meredith and John Garfield, né Julius
Garfinkle. By July, when *We Will Never Die* reached the West

Franz Waxman conducts, Hollywood Bowl

Coast, with an especially lavish production at the Hollywood
Bowl, Akim Tamiroff, Joan Leslie, Paul Henreid, and Edward
Arnold had been recruited, and the souvenir program included
testimonials from Thomas Mann, Dorothy Parker, and Sinclair Lewis ("Ben Hecht . . . has devoted all of his training and
shrewd craftsmanship, along with his deep love of liberty and
human dignity, so that we have not a somewhat boresome spectacle, but one with all the thrills of a Wagnerian opera. Here
is one of the first examples of the great art that should, but
scarcely has yet, come out of the War for Democracy.") The
memorial's honorary chairmen included everyone from studio
heads Mayer, Goldwyn, Selznick, Harry Cohn, Joseph Schenck,
and Jack and Harry Warner to Governor Earl Warren, William Randolph Hearst, both the mayor and the archbishop of
Los Angeles, and Edgar Magnin, rabbi to the stars. Composer
Franz Waxman and lyricist Frank Loesser added a stirring "Battle Hymn of the Ghetto," with which the production closed:
"We the *scum of human chattel*/We of everlasting flight/We
will rise in fearless battle/We who cannot live the night . . ."

Rabbi Wise and his supporters had, meanwhile, also exerted a great deal of effort in their own historic campaign—and
had managed successfully to block the staging of the memorial
in Baltimore, Buffalo, Rochester, and Kingston, New York, as
well as Gary, Indiana.

9

The Flag

THE REACTIONS of Hecht's old friends to his new fixation
on the Jews ranged wildly—from derision to perplexity to fer-
vent support. H. L. Mencken, for one, fairly oozed contempt
and blamed Hecht's time in very Jewish Hollywood for having taken "the sting out of the American Rabelais" and driven
him "back to the ghetto." In 1939, according to the not exactly
philo-Semitic Mencken, one of the founders of the magazine
he mentions here, Hecht's "congenital Jewishness began to
dominate him, and by February 1943, he was contributing to
the *American Mercury* (now owned and run by Jews) a set of
prose dithyrambs upon the woes of Israel, fit almost for recit-
ing at the Wailing Wall."

Charlie MacArthur, on the other hand, was more baffled
than anything—and maybe a little jealous. MacArthur "used to
pester the hell out of me," Bergson would later recall. "Because,
he says, 'Ben was never with any cause more than six weeks. And

I was waiting for the six weeks to pass . . . and you son of a bitch, it's now five years. How did you do it?' "

MacArthur was probably ascribing more power to Bergson than he really had over Hecht, who wasn't, after all, some helpless hypnotist's subject. And despite his insistence that "the rescue of the word Jew from the garbage can into which the Germans had dumped it" had been his singular goal throughout these years, both the "cause" and Hecht's approach to it kept mutating, which helped to hold his always flickering attention. Soon after the somber splash made by *We Will Never Die*, in fact, he shifted gears dramatically—moving from the grand, earnest, collaborative realm of the mass memorial to writing a quirky, angry, funny, and very personal meditation-cum-diatribe, into which he had resolved to "put . . . the little of what I knew about Jews and the great deal that I knew about their enemies." With an emphasis on the latter.

A Guide for the Bedevilled was dashed off in a gleeful white heat during the summer of 1943, just as Rose was reaching term, then giving birth to their daughter, Jenny, a fact he marveled at. ("I am about to become a father—not a grandfather, which is comparatively easy—" the fifty-year-old Hecht had written Gene Fowler earlier that year, ". . . a genuine youthful parent. Without the aid of test tubes, bicycle pumps, or other scientific devices.") Hecht's polemic is another curious document, one whose scattershot and none-too-Maimonidean structure he admits at the outset. "I am not," he explains, "writing a book that is already in my head. I am investigating publicly, exposing my mind spontaneously to the reader, and I am a little alarmed at the disorder in store for him." The book is indeed a full-fledged mess, but an ecstatic one—with all the gall and the gusto of which he was capable. As he writes "of Jews with love and of their enemies with hatred," he careens from bilious disquisitions on the anti-Semitism of Voltaire, Hilaire Belloc, and a Yale sociology professor named Kennedy to chortling homages to figures like Abraham Aboulafia, the medieval kabbalist who aspired to convert the pope to Judaism. Hecht's darkly whimsical historical gallivanting is punctuated by periodic ad hominem assaults on "the Germans," who, he writes, "outraged me because they are murderers, foul and wanton, and because they are fools such as gibber at a roadside, with spittle running from their mouths. They outraged me because they raised little pig eyes to their betters and sought to grunt and claw their way to the mastery of men. They outraged me because they fouled the name even of war, fouled the hopes of men, fouled a generation that belonged to me. And they outraged me because I am a Jew."

But here, in that little pronoun, was the key to the book's raw vitality: Hecht could rant all he wanted about "the German" with "his fat neck, his watery eyes, and his faded skin"; he could coax from his reading of Heinrich Graetz's multivolume *History of the Jews* fanciful riffs on the trials and tenacity of its title characters throughout the ages. He was, though, at his most nuanced and believable when he set out to examine his memories of being Jewish on the Lower East Side, in Racine, Chicago, Berlin, New York, and Hollywood. For mixed in with the fairly exhausting crazy quilt of invective and error-ridden anecdote that make up the *Guide* is Hecht's sharpest autobiographical writing to date. While for years he'd been using his own experiences as grist for novels, stories, newspaper columns, plays, and even the occasional Hollywood script, this book marks the birth of Hecht the memoirist. It was in many ways the role that best suited his blackly comic prose-writing self, and it's striking that the subject of his relationship to his Jewishness—and to his Americanness, as a Jew—is what first brought this persona to the fore, as though admitting the compound nature of his own identity had uncorked his ability to reckon directly with the whole of his intricate being. "I doubt equally whether I am I, the Jew, or We, the Americans," he muses in his *Guide*. "I could make out a case for myself as either or neither, which is another way of saying that I am both."

While Mencken might have scowled and MacArthur scratched his head, other friends appreciated what Hecht was trying to do. "Notwithstanding the brilliance of your work in the past," Fowler wrote him in late August, "I have known all along that you were one day going to excel yourself. That is quite a big order, for I think you have done the finest writing of our time, and no one for the last fifty years at least has bobbed up fully armed with words as you have done. In this book that you are doing, I know, sight unseen, that you are striking with the power of Thor on the anvil of your great gift."

However hyperbolic that praise may have been, the completed manuscript did instantly stir the interest of legendary Scribner's editor Maxwell Perkins, who, he wrote Hecht, "wanted to publish 'The Guide' the moment I saw it, just on principle, and then very much more after I had read it for its fire and power as literature." Once Scribner's had issued the book in March of 1944—"under wartime conditions," as the copyright page put it with inadvertent irony—Perkins continued to defend it against the usual strong reactions that Hecht's work provoked. And from those within Hecht's own circle the *Guide* drew predictable kudos, with Bergson and Merlin, Samuel Goldwyn and Edward G. Robinson sending high praise, as did Hecht's close Berlin companion George Grosz, whom he singles out in the book as an exemplary "German orphan"—that is, a virtuous exception to the bloodthirsty Teutonic type he'd set out to skewer: "Dear Benny," wrote Grosz, now living in exile on Long Island, "this is just to let you know how much I enjoyed reading your last book . . . nay, enjoying is not the right word, because it is full of bitternis [*sic*] and stirs up all the old wounds . . . so cleverly covered up by most of us. . . . It is a great crusading book I might say."

But even a crusader needs a promoter, a part Billy Rose

seemed happy to play—negotiating with Perkins to print extra copies despite paper shortages and the apparent reluctance on the part of others at the publishing house who were, Rose explained, "frankly alarmed at the prospect of being deluged with calls for this book." He also lobbied the *New York Post* to serialize it, and Walter Winchell to plug it ("more devastating for Nazis than any weapon yet," declared the unflaggingly scrappy radio and newspaper personality)—and by early May "the box score," as Rose called the best-seller list, included the book. In just two months Scribner's had, he reported to Hecht, "disposed of over 17,000 copies. . . . This of course is encouraging considering that your book is not a Jewish obituary notice."

The critics, meanwhile, offered passionate if mixed reactions to this passionately mixed-up book. The *New York Times* described it as "lusty, coruscating . . . partly an attack on anti-Semitism and partly a bit of inspired biography," though the reviewer suggested, rightly, that "the only thing that is wrong with Ben Hecht's book is that it is too angry to remember that the Germans, even as the English, the French and the Jews, are a racial amalgam of Nordic, Mediterranean, Asiatic and Alpine stocks, a higgledy-piggledy mixture that is no more 'Aryan' than Ben Hecht, Clark Gable or Duke Kohanomoku of Hawaii. . . . [His] is a sort of anti-Semitism turned inside out. I don't blame Ben Hecht for being angry at the bestiality of the modern Germans. . . . But should anger cause one to take leave of one's senses? Isn't it dangerous to become the image of your enemy, a bump to his hollow, an equal and opposite reaction to his false reading of history?"

Others were much harsher, with the Judaica professor–to–be Ben Halpern fulminating in the *New Leader* against what he called Hecht's "abysmal ignorance of Jewish history and utter indifference to real, living Jews. . . . This book is not written about the Jews. It was written about Ben Hecht."

Halpern had a point—and while for him, this self-absorption was a mark of failure, for other readers Hecht's response to anti-Semitism as an acutely personal affront was precisely the source of its power. Dedicated to "Jenny, Aged 3 Days," this wasn't an academic tract or reasoned argument, so much as a furious *cri de coeur* crossed with a frenzied *J'accuse*. . . . Oddly, it was Hecht himself who would echo Halpern's words when he began to wonder, in the wake of the book's publication and his growing frustration with the work of the Committee, whether "the cause I had tried to serve was even sensible. Did such a cause even exist—the salvaging of the word Jew? What did it mean? Obviously one of its meanings was the fact that my ego had identified itself with this historic word. Something in me, as well as in Europe, was being removed and befouled. Since it had always been my habit to answer insults, I had answered back to the Germans. But was an outraged ego a cause?" He was, he announced, finished with propaganda.

Until, that is, he wasn't. Following Hecht's violent shifts and starts throughout this period can give one a case of ideological motion sickness, as he lurched from position to position—explaining the movement from stance to stance with eloquent if not quite crystalline logic. Though he doubted his own motives and had begun to see the Bergsonites' campaign as largely ineffectual (he seemed to agree with Kurt Weill's assessment of their pageant's impact: "All we have done is make a lot of Jews cry, which is not a unique accomplishment"), it was at just this time that their work started to bear modest fruit. While Hecht had been writing his *Guide*—as well as welcoming baby Jenny into the world, buying a second home, on the beach, in Oceanside, California, composing a treacly and weirdly Christological novella called *Miracle in the Rain*, and whipping off a satirical Hollywood murder mystery, *I Hate Actors!*—Bergson had continued to lobby and organize. A few days before Yom Kippur, 1943, he'd staged a symbolically potent march of some four hundred Orthodox rabbis on Washington, where they delivered a petition to Vice President Henry Wallace, demanding the creation of a governmental agency to save "the remnant of the people of the Book" in Europe. (FDR slid out on "other business" when he heard the rabbis were coming.) Working with various sympathetic senators and representatives, Bergson had managed to introduce the notion of such an agency to Congress, in the form of a "rescue resolution." And in the wake of a gathering of Allied leaders in Moscow that fall, Hecht wrote and the Committee published another attention-grabbing ad in multiple newspapers. Adopting the voice of his imaginary Uncle Abraham, a ghost who spoke for the murdered millions, Hecht decried the absence of the word *Jew* from the "statement of atrocities," signed at the close of the Russian conference. Why, the specter wondered, were Stalin, Roosevelt, and Churchill "afraid to speak of us. . . . We were not allowed by the Germans to stay alive. We are not allowed by the Four Freedoms to be dead." The avuncular ghost, wrote Hecht, was now haunting the White House, where he sat on "a window sill two feet away from Mr. Roosevelt."

While it's doubtful that these words themselves were what finally brought about FDR's move to try and protect the Jews of Europe, he was said to be particularly disturbed by Hecht's spooky ad, and it seems to have helped goad him into action. By mid-January of 1944, when treasury secretary Henry Morgenthau Jr. presented Roosevelt with the précis of a stinging dossier prepared by a group of officials in his own department, "Report to the Secretary on the Acquiescence of This Government in the Murder of the Jews," the president was at last ready, and within a few weeks he issued an executive order establishing the War Refugee Board, whose official mandate was "to take all measures within its power to rescue the victims of enemy oppression who are in imminent danger of death." This wasn't "mere . . . lipservice," as Billy Rose put it in a letter to Hecht soon after. It may have been too little too late, but "it's the first thing stripped of abracadabra."

Although anti-Semitism is the primary preoccupation of the *Guide*, Hecht shifts gears abruptly at the book's close and launches into a plainspoken dialogue between "the author" and "his conscience" on the question of Palestine and the "efforts of the Jews to build for themselves a nation in that land."

The author declares that these efforts are "admirable" and that the solution to the European Jewish problem "may well lie in their success." His conscience points out that he has remained curiously silent about the matter till now, which the author concedes, admitting that he has been torn. "I would be glad to see a nation of Jews under a Jewish flag, and I am sure that such a nation would perform valorously and importantly on the world stage. Yet I have no impulse to contribute anything of myself to its existence. . . . When I contemplate a Jewish state I become something I have never been before—an exile." He goes on: "My silence is not an argument against a Palestinian homeland but an honesty toward the dreams of others. . . . Palestine does not need abstracted champions like myself. It needs heroes with the smell of its soil in their noses; heroes with the word Jew stamped in their souls, and not hanging on them like a tag."

Given the unequivocal nature of that statement, what, then, would cause him to suddenly pivot—and become just such an abstracted champion? While for some time Hecht continued to insist that this wasn't his fight to fight, he would soon emerge as one of the most devoted, vociferous, downright bellicose American supporters of the foundation of a Jewish state in Palestine. Of Hecht's many shifts of tack and tone, this is among the most jarring, and confusing.

Whether or not one agrees in hindsight with the strategies

adopted by Bergson, Merlin, and their Revisionist-minded comrades, it's not hard to grasp in both emotional and intellectual terms the evolution of these Palestinian Irgun activists from tireless rescue workers into tireless Zionist campaigners. Even before the war's end, they had shifted their focus from Europe to the Middle East, and had pledged support for the revolt declared in February 1944 by the Irgun's commander, Menachem Begin. Though Begin and his forces had launched an all-out armed uprising, aimed at driving the British from Palestine, while Bergson and his men saw their American mission as primarily political, the two causes were obviously linked. In May of that year, the Bergsonites had signaled this change of emphasis by giving their organization yet another new name—the Hebrew Committee of National Liberation—and pooling the money they'd raised in the United States to buy an imposing mansion, formerly the Iranian embassy, on Washington's Massachusetts Avenue. Declaring this their unofficial embassy, they had announced their intention to seek U.N. recognition for the embryonic Hebrew Nation and hoisted the blue and white "flag of Judah" in front of the grand Beaux-Arts building.

But what was all this to Ben Hecht? Not only had he repeatedly declared Palestine far beyond his American purview, the very emphasis on the word *Hebrew*, as opposed to *Jew*, would seem to exclude him and all his tender memories of long-dead tantes and uncles from this particular conversation. "It is," declared Bergson at the time of the founding of this latest Committee, picking up and varying ideas formulated by a small group of radical European and Palestinian intellectuals known as the Canaanites, "essential to maintain the clear distinction between Hebrews, who are people belonging to a specific national and political entity—the Hebrew Nation—and the 'Jewish People,' which is a religious and ethnic entity. 'Jewish people' can be Americans, Russians, Britons, etc. Hebrews can be but one thing—*Hebrews*." Though the vocabulary would shift after

1948, he was essentially laying the groundwork for the separation of synagogue and state that he hoped would prevail in the brand-new country he was fighting to establish. According to Bergson's decidedly maverick vision, Israelis would be one thing, and Jews, another.

It seems unlikely that Hecht the consummate word man failed to notice the gap between those terms. Wiring Bergson to commend him on the creation of the new Committee, he wrote that "the Jewish cause has been too long under the domination of people like Stephen Wise and his fellow Jewish fossils. What the Jews need most is a high wind to blow these ossified politicos out of their places. They are the dust that has gathered over a lost cause." He made no mention of Hebrews— though neither did he offer to sign up for this latest iteration of the cause. And when, soon after, Bergson and Merlin visited him, in hopes of persuading him to lend a hand in this next stage of their struggle, he dismissed them caustically: "If you want to start a country . . . go find Washington or Bolivar or Garibaldi. And go dig up Nathan Hale and Robert Bruce, Robert Emmet and Joan of Arc. There are no such characters living in Nyack." Declaring himself done with the matter, he announced that "I'll write no more propaganda babble about Jews."

And yet—there he was, just a short time later, reporting for duty at the Committee's New York office (which itself had a freshly painted name on the door, the American League for a Free Palestine, a clever if slightly sneaky way of making room for non-"Hebrew" supporters of the cause), and proclaiming, as he quoted himself in his memoir, returning to a familiar motif: "I'll start writing about Jews again. Imagine reading of a Jewish battle instead of a pogrom!"

Besides acknowledging his usual preference for battle over almost any other activity, how best to understand this drastic change of heart, and the fact that Hecht would soon become one very vocal cochairman of that same American League for a

Free Palestine? Was it simply his need to keep startling his own system by veering in *this* direction then, without warning, *that?* Or did this sudden urge to propagandize on behalf of the Irgun represent his lifelong romanticization of tough guys—gangsters, boxers, thugs—pumped up on nationalistic steroids? (Bergson may have been consumed with rallying international political support for the establishment of a provisional Palestinian government; to Hecht, the idea of a down-and-dirty physical brawl was much more alluring. Playfully connecting this national liberation struggle against the British with that of the Irish, he'd once signed a telegram to Bergsonite supporter Senator Guy Gillette "Ben McHecht," as he issued up a rousing: "Up MacBergson! Up MacGillette! Up Michael O'Ben-Ami!") He had an uncanny knack for placing himself wherever the action was. Perhaps he sensed the warmth of another historical hot spot and had gravitated instinctively in its direction. Or maybe he viewed this crusade as one more chance to stand up to a bully or bullies. Besides fighting the British and the strict limits they'd placed on Jewish immigration to Palestine—the illegal "repatriation" of European displaced persons to Palestine became a central aspect of the Committee's work at this stage—the Bergsonites were still fending off attacks by a host of powerful mainstream American Jewish organizations, who publicly denounced what they called "an insignificantly small, pistol-packing group of extremists who are claiming credit for the recent terror outrages" as they continued to wage a relentless behind-the-scenes campaign to deport or draft, audit, investigate, and harass by any means possible Bergson and his cadre.

Or was Hecht's newfound commitment to valorizing the violent revolt in Palestine a function of something more desperate, basic, and compensatory—blind rage at his own impotence in the face of the European bloodbath? For all their efforts, he, the Committee, and the rest of the world hadn't, in the end, managed to halt it. Had his anguish at the knowledge

Opening night

of that fact transformed his sometimes fanciful, rhetorical fury into this call to very actual arms?

Whatever the complex and even contradictory brew of motivations fueling him, once Hecht had joined up again, he left no room for the slightest doubt about his beliefs or the ferocity with which he held them. The result was his least subtle and most immediately effective propaganda effort to date, an unambiguous piece of pro-Irgun agitprop, called in a preliminary draft *Palestine Is Ours* and by September 5, 1946, when it opened for a limited run at Broadway's Alvin Theater, retitled *A Flag Is Born*.

With music by Kurt Weill, directed by Luther Adler, starring Paul Muni, Celia Adler, and a relatively unknown twenty-two-year-old non-Jewish actor who had come highly recommended by the Adler family, Marlon Brando, the play opened onto what the narrator (journalist Quentin Reynolds) described as "a woebegone graveyard that has seen better days." The symbolism was obvious: Europe had become one large Jewish cemetery. "Two Jews, two remnant Jews of Europe plod slowly the dark night," the narrator intoned. "Their feet drag, for they carry a heavy burden. Their hearts are like stones that read 'a dead world lies here.'" In this pointedly melodramatic scheme, whose broad emotional strokes seem drawn from the Yiddish theater—where Muni and the Adlers got their start, and which first thrilled Hecht as a child when he'd sat among the chicken-chomping spectators, watching their father, Jacob Adler, performing in *The Kreutzer Sonata*—the gray-bearded Tevya and kerchiefed Zelda are meant to represent an old-fashioned, trusting, and, to Hecht's mind, now-necrotic way of being Jewish. (In that earlier draft, Zelda's name had been Goldie, as in the Sholom Aleichem stories that Hecht had long loved, though this script seemed to mark the end of his affair with the sort of gently pious, good-natured, and fundamentally powerless Jewish characters in whom the great Yiddish writer specialized.) As this couple of ancient-seeming Treblinka survivors trudge, they are, the narrator explains, "moving toward a land of love, of milk and honey, of holy song—called Palestine."

But Tevya and Zelda are, it's clear, too tired, too weak, too soft with shtetl sentiment to complete the grueling physical and psychic journey. That difficult, transformative trip will be left to a "gaunt and grim-looking" young Jew, David (Brando), whom they meet en route and who has "the cold look of a lord high executioner. His eighteen years wear a face that has sat in judgment of life and condemned it." A set of biblically fraught visions follow—populated by Kings Saul, David, and Solomon, "sandaled women, garlanded and lovely . . . robed priests," and the couple's multiple dead children—and Tevya addresses a U.N.-like Council of the Mighty, before whom he implores, "open one little door for the Jews who have opened so many

Brando, Celia Adler, Muni

big doors for everybody else. Open one little door to Palestine,
to Eretz Yisrael." The mighty statesmen agree to put the matter
on "tomorrow's agenda," and adjourn their session with knowing laughter, at which the Brando character bitterly mocks
Tevya for "holding out his heart like a beggar's cap! . . . With
whom are you pleading there, Tevya? . . . The dead and the liv-

ing have the same ears for the Jews—dead ears." Zelda succumbs to her fatigue and despair, and when Tevya too collapses under what seems the weight of the ages, David is poised to kill himself—"Of what use is a man in darkness? Of what use is a Jew in a world of poison and shame?"—but as he lifts the knife to do himself in, he's summoned by a sort of Greek chorus of Hebrew soldiers, crying: "Don't you hear our guns, David? We battle the English—the sly and powerful English. We speak to them in a new Jewish language, the language of guns. We fling no more prayers or tears at the world. We fling bullets. We fling barrages." In the final moments, David takes the dead Tevya's prayer shawl, cuts off its fringes, affixes a blue star to its middle, and hoists this makeshift flag on a branch high above him. "Hatikva" plays and, as the stage directions have it, the young man "walks toward the light, the singing and the sound of guns . . ."

The blatant nature of the message was, of course, intentional—the published version of the script featured an introduction by the Rumanian-born writer Konrad Bercovici, who praised the drama as "a propaganda play—frankly and deliberately"—and its purpose was threefold. First, it aimed at a kind of catharsis, which it certainly achieved: Brando later remembered the scene in which his character faced the audience and cried, "Where were you—Jews? Where were you when the killing was going on?" And as he bellowed, "at some performances Jewish girls got out of their seats and screamed and cried from the aisles in sadness." One night, as he gave this speech, a woman was "so overcome with anger and guilt she rose and shouted back at me, 'Where were *you?*'"

The other two goals were stated plainly in the press materials, which explained that the play "was not written to amuse or to beguile. [It] was written to make money—to make money to provide ships to get Hebrews to Palestine . . . and . . . [to] arouse American public opinion to support the fight for freedom and independence now being waged by the resistance in Palestine."

And these aims, too, it achieved. *A Flag Is Born* had originally been scheduled to play on Broadway for just four weeks, but popular demand was such that the run was extended for several extra months, it eventually toured the country, and, despite the tremendous range of critical opinion—"colorful theater and biting propaganda," *Time* enthused; "a turgid stage polemic," the *New York Times* complained—it created something of a sensation, with noisy protests taking place before packed houses. As Rose Hecht later summed up the response, "many Jews picketed . . . and many Jews came and wept." The play also raised a great deal of money. After just a month, in fact, the proceeds from ticket sales, donations, and loans based on the projection of future profits were such that the Committee was able to wire nearly a quarter of a million dollars to Europe, to help lay the foundation for the provisional government. It also had enough cash on hand to buy a rusting former German luxury yacht at an American government surplus auction. Though the craft was described by one witness as "just about ready for the scrap pile," it would do.

As always, the Bergsonite idea was both to act and to call dramatic attention to that acting. The plan was to man the boat with an all-American volunteer crew before bringing as many illegal "Hebrew" immigrants as possible on board in Europe. In doing so, the Committee hoped to force the British to arrest American citizens, then challenge their actions in Palestinian courts and in the court of world opinion. So it was that on December 26, 1946, after the FBI searched the boat for arms and found only lifejackets and provisions—flour, fruit juice, and sixteen hundred pounds of salami—the creaky old S.S. *Abril* set sail from Staten Island, and, after a stormy crossing, arrived six days behind schedule at Port-de-Bouc, near Marseilles. Flying a Honduran flag, allegedly bound for Bolivia, and carrying a crew of twenty (seven of them non-Jews who'd signed on, in the words of one of them, because he "didn't like to see a minority kicked around"), along with 625 Jewish displaced persons, two reporters, and a photographer, the boat set sail again on February 28, 1947. As soon as it passed out of French territorial waters, cheers and "Hatikva" went up on deck as one of the commanders proclaimed the new name of the vessel, heading to Palestine: he called it the S.S. *Ben Hecht.*

10

The Child

UNABASHEDLY BLUNT, utterly subtle—Hecht had always gone both ways, and now this game of tonal tug-of-war played out more violently within him than ever. Just months before he wrote the placardlike *A Flag Is Born* and began issuing up bald financial appeals on behalf of the Irgun ("IT TAKES GUTS! . . . Words won't carry the Hebrews to Palestine. Ships will. Give us the money—it will get the ships," read one of his Bergsonite ads from this period), he was working hard to fashion a script so shrewd it would soon evolve into the film François Truffaut came to call "truly my favorite Hitchcock picture . . . the very quintessence of Hitchcock."

Notorious isn't just a sexy, darkly sophisticated romantic thriller in which a dashing government agent (Cary Grant) recruits the party-girl daughter of a convicted Nazi spy (Ingrid Bergman) to seduce a family friend (Claude Rains) and so infiltrate a band of German operatives in Brazil. Hecht and Hitchcock had collaborated the year before on the psychoanalytic melodrama *Spellbound* and also worked on a short documentary for the State Department and Office of War Information, *Watchtower over Tomorrow*, about the founding of the United Nations. Now they imbued their would-be escapist film with a fiendishly effective dose of the period's deepest anxieties. Besides those scheming Nazis on the loose in Rio (they are employees of the Zyklon-B-producing I. G. Farben company, no less), the film's plot involves federal wiretapping, the menace of female sexual control (and lack of control), and, most topical for its moment, uranium ore, stashed secretly in wine bottles. Despite the glib insistence of both screenwriter and director that this detail had been a mere MacGuffin, such a twist concocted right around the month when the United States dropped bombs on Hiroshima and Nagasaki couldn't possibly have been as random or trivial as that. Although the director later claimed that, well before August 1945, he and Hecht had consulted a prominent Caltech physicist about the dimensions of a theoretical hydrogen bomb—alarming the Nobel winner with their questions about top-secret matters—it isn't clear whether this meeting really took place. They continued to revise the script through the autumn, so the atomic particulars might well have been introduced *after* that terrible nuclear summer. But no matter when that headline-worthy touch came to be, Hecht's taut dialogue and Hitchcock's leering camerawork together create a distinct psychological urgency and raised dramatic pulse that gave the picture—still give it—the resonance of an all-too-timely nightmare. Moral compromise, sexual suspicion, and slow-seeping poison permeate the film, in which no one, nothing, can be trusted, even one's own prejudices. And in this sense too that uranium seems more than any old MacGuffin: it was, according to Hitchcock, "an unstable element, just like the world." Even the always-assured Hecht seemed uneasy about certain former certainties. While just recently his *Guide for the Bedev-*

illed had blasted the Germans in the most unambiguous and categorical terms, now he'd created in the Claude Rains character something genuinely shocking—a sensitive, vulnerable, and almost sympathetic Nazi.

This was just one of the contradictions that pervaded his work during these years, as he continued to dash off scripts that ranged from sincere attempts at artistic expression to shameless pandering for paychecks. In late 1945 he wrote, directed, and produced a slight if heartfelt comic drama about ballet and business, madness and murder, *Specter of the Rose*. Shot and co-directed by Lee Garmes, with music by George Antheil and starring Judith Anderson, Michael Chekhov, and Lionel Stander (once again doing his best growling Bodenheim imitation), the movie is by turns winning and grating, unfolding as it does in the intimate, playful mode of the Astoria pictures and sometimes giving way to a sort of arty heavy breathing that's hard to know how to take. As with those earlier productions, the film's charms are in large part verbal, its attitude wry and insiderish. This led some to dismiss it as merely pretentious, with one critic accusing the picture and Hecht of "so much drab Bohemianism." That assessment, though, doesn't seem fair to a movie that takes such pleasure in poking gentle fun at its characters' theatrical affectations. On entering a barre-and-ballerina-filled studio, for instance, the two-bit impresario played by the quietly delightful Chekhov (nephew of Anton, student of Stanislavski, teacher of Marilyn Monroe) flutters his lashes, flares his nostrils, and declares in a Russian accent that's real but sounds half make-believe, "Oh, the smell of art! The lovely smell of art!"

In general, it was money that made Hecht's own writerly nose twitch most noticeably these days. Over the next year he would polish the script for Charles Vidor's *Gilda*, help Selznick tinker with his hopelessly souped-up, exhaust-spewing *Duel in the Sun*, and, working at what had become known as his "Oceanside factory," crank out at least another seven scripts. These ranged from a rewrite of Hitchcock's unusually stilted court-room drama, *The Paradine Case* (which Hecht doctored on condition that his name not appear in the credits), to two neat noirs written with Lederer, *Ride the Pink Horse* (for Robert Montgomery) and *Kiss of Death* (for Henry Hathaway). This couple of lean, mean gangster pictures emerged from Hecht's crowded head as, together with animator and gag writer Frank Tashlin, he was sketching out *Diamonds in the Pavement*, a largely silent vehicle for his old friend Harpo Marx; that film would later be retooled crudely by various hands and emerge rather unhappily as the last Marx Brothers movie, *Love Happy*. Meanwhile, Hecht phoned in the Lucille Ball comedy *Her Husband's Affairs*, a strained and not very funny proto–*I Love Lucy*, minus Desi, and he collaborated with Quentin Reynolds on an adaptation of the mawkish best seller *The Miracle of the Bells*. This, on condition that Reynolds read the novel and report back to Hecht, who couldn't bear to do it himself. "I just can't," he explained. "It's a hunk of junk." The *New York Times* felt the same about the movie that resulted, naming it one of the worst pictures of the year: "We . . . assume that Ben Hecht and Quentin Reynolds are willing to divide the dead cats and overripe tomatoes that will be flung, from certain quarters, at the script."

Although Hecht had long been expert at compartmentalization—able to draft these wildly variable sorts of screenplays even as he carried on with his earnest literary efforts and propagandized for the Irgun—others proved increasingly reluctant to distinguish between Hecht the hack, Hecht the artist, and Hecht the political firebrand. And it was at the same time he was both leaping at any opportunity to denounce "the sly British" and working (very amicably) with Hitchcock, a sly Brit if there ever was one, that these various roles collided.

Since he and the Committee had shifted attention from rescue in Europe to "repatriation" and armed rebellion in Palestine, Hecht had ramped up his attacks on the "British hooligans" and those who would excuse their policies in the Middle East. And since the March 8, 1947, capture of the S.S. *Ben Hecht* by the royal navy—which took place just as the Committee had expected, with two British destroyers intercepting the boat off the Palestine coast, sending the passengers to DP camps in Cyprus, and imprisoning the crew in Haifa—his rhetoric had grown fiercer. The crew was eventually released and deported, and at a banquet held in the sailors' honor at New York's Astor Hotel in late April that year, Hecht gave a speech in which he reviled both the "English rascals and hypocrites" and those "Jews who imagine that if they are seen crawling on their bellies they will be mistaken for non-Jews or at least high class Jews. I'm thinking," he explained, "of a White Christmas named Arthur Sulzberger . . . [whose] stomach-tour among the Anglo-Saxons is not a new spectacle in Jewish history." Praising instead the "Jewish patriots . . . who went into battle armed only with—another cheek to be slapped," he moved once more into his unabashedly blunt mode and declared that whereas until recently "there were some fifty-seven varieties of Palestinian strategists, Zionist Palaverers and Hebrew disputants . . . today there are only two Jewish parties left in the field—the Terrorists—and the Terrified."

Which left little doubt about which side he was on, a fact he trumpeted still more stridently when, several weeks later, he and the Committee issued up their most provocative ad yet. Running twice in the *New York Post* and once in the *Herald Tribune* that May, this full-page proclamation, signed by Hecht, announced itself a

Letter to the Terrorists of Palestine

"My brave friends," it began. "*You may not believe what I write you, for there is a lot of fertilizer in the air at the moment.*

"But on my word as an old reporter, what I write is true.

"The Jews of America are for you. You are their champions. You are the grin they wear. You are the feather in their hats . . ." and so on, with a bit more slangy, macho buildup, till he fired off the paragraph that would become the most famous—or infamous—he ever wrote:

"Every time you blow up a British arsenal, or wreck a British jail, or send a British railroad train sky high, or rob a British bank or let go with your guns and bombs at the British betrayers and invaders of your homeland, the Jews of America make a little holiday in their hearts."

Highly perverse even by Hechtian standards, this verbal Molotov cocktail was obviously hurled with intent to inflame. As always, Hecht relished playing the bad boy, and while he must have understood the anger these words would prompt, it isn't clear he'd considered the effect that widespread outrage might have on his own livelihood. Others had been concerned about the incendiary tenor of the ad from the outset—not for such pragmatic reasons but as a matter of principle. It was one thing to howl in righteous indignation as the Nazis butchered millions of European Jews and the American government looked on; it was quite another to crow ecstatically over the use of terror—even against an occupying power whose policies you considered criminal. Disturbed by Hecht's words, Merlin for one had urged Bergson to scrap the ad before it ran. Bergson thought it fine (though would later regret having published it—not because he didn't agree with the sentiments expressed there but because he came to consider it "bad propaganda"). Merlin was far from alone in his opposition, as the reaction was instantaneous and overwhelmingly hostile: an Associated Press article syndicated in multiple U.S. papers described Hecht as "an American whose name was scarcely known to the British public a few weeks ago [but who had become] Public Villain No. 1 to the British press." This same wire story quoted the English *Evening Standard* as accusing him of "gross Chauvinism, distortion of history, indoctrination of children, preference of solutions through violence, race pride, the stoking up of hatred between nations, indifference to the sanctity of human life." The *Daily Mail* condemned him as a "vitriolic Zionist volcano with a touch of the carnival huckster," and the British ambassador to the United States even lodged a formal complaint with the American State Department, describing Hecht's advertisement as nothing short of "incitement to murder."

While President Truman responded with a tame statement, urging United States citizens to refrain from any activities that might further rouse "the passions of the inhabitants of Palestine," the American reaction was generally just as antagonistic as the English had been. Walter Winchell did come to Hecht's defense, dubbing the British "the Brutish" and likening the "Palestinian patriots" to "our Minute Men," but Hecht was widely vilified for the ad, which Nahum Goldmann, a leading figure in the American Zionist establishment, denounced as "disgusting." The Chicago-born novelist and liberal Zionist Meyer Levin—who'd once looked up to Hecht and even sought out his literary advice as a young man—decried the "little holiday in their hearts" line by writing in terms that share with Hecht's own a certain hot-headed hyperbole: "I don't believe any single phrase was ever more harmful to the Jewish people."

Meanwhile, Hecht's old friend Herman Mankiewicz summed up the situation most efficiently, perhaps, when asked about why Hecht had become so radical a Zionist, advocating violence: "It's very simple," he reportedly said. "You see, six years ago Ben found out that he was a Jew, and now he behaves like a six-year-old Jew."

But why, really, had he done it? Had Hecht genuinely meant that bloodthirsty battle cry—or was this yet another gambit by the preternaturally facile wordmeister to see whether he could make something significant *happen* with his writing?

In fact, the ad's publication did have real consequences, though, again, it seems unlikely that he'd anticipated the harsh and personal form they would take. And first there had been cheering signs of popular support. These had come in the wake of a near-death experience he'd had that summer, when an operation to remove gallstones revealed peritonitis, necessitating multiple surgeries. ("A sort of Japanese rock garden [was] needlessly ornamenting my interior," Hecht wrote Gene Fowler from the hospital, to which his friend replied that "it must have been a novelty to have had the knife in your front instead of your back for a change.") When Hecht returned home to Nyack, he found letters, "barrels of them, and they were from Jews." These tributes "brought tears to me—" he wrote, "particularly the misspelled ones full of the sort of odd grammar my parents had favored in their correspondence. The epistles from the educated were almost as moving. The love in all of them was a tonic that made my sawed-up insides feel firm again."

On the other hand, much sterner assessments were also in the offing—the effects of which Hecht did nothing to soften by continuing, even in his convalescence, to loudly laud the Irgun's most murderous actions. Answering a call put to him by none other than Menachem Begin (who wrote Hecht under a nom de guerre that June and thanked him for having stood at "our side without fear or compromise, and . . . [having] shown readiness to take the stones hurled at you from all sides"), he conceived yet another propaganda play. In terms still more schematic and morbidly sentimental than *A Flag Is Born*, this resuscitated the figures of both Tevya and the medieval Hebrew poet Jehuda Halevy to celebrate the life and armed struggle of Dov Gruner, an Irgun fighter hanged by the British earlier that year. Running for several nights that September at Carnegie Hall, it was titled *The Terrorist*—a word Hecht seemed now as fixated on flaunting as he'd once been on the mention of "Jews." It was because of provocations like this that one night at around this time Hecht and Mankiewicz let rip a shouting match, during which Herman accused Ben of "making me an alien in my own country." Their friendship somehow survived this scotch-fueled standoff, but the argument typified the profound anxiety, not to say anger, Hecht had stirred among many of his peers, even those to whom he was closest.

By December, he was well enough to travel back to the West Coast, where he enlisted the help of the mobster Mickey Cohen to raise more money for the Irgun. Hecht later described first meeting the squat Los Angeles crime boss when he turned up at Hecht's Oceanside home, "to inquire of me what he could do to help the Jewish cause in Palestine." Cohen and the henchmen who arrived with him in a bulletproof limousine that day didn't take off their hats, and, as the amazed screenwriter of *Underworld* and *Scarface* put it, "They acted like people I made up." (Cohen himself claimed that Hecht had been the one to seek *him* out and that he hadn't then known who the writer was—"there might have been a lot about him in the papers . . . but the difference was that he could read and I couldn't too well.") At a packed fund-raising dinner that Cohen hosted at Slapsy Maxie's Café on Wilshire Boulevard that winter, Hecht managed—despite his weakened, postoperative state—to deliver a lengthy and spirited address to a nightclub filled with "a thousand bookies, ex-prize fighters, gamblers, jockeys, touts and all sorts of lawless and semi-lawless characters; and their womenfolk." Designed to help this thuggish crew identify with "the soldiers of the Irgun who fought with a British noose around their necks," the speech extolled those who for years "were called gangsters and terrorists, pirates and law breakers. . . . But . . . history has revealed them in their true guise—not that of Terrorists but of champions risen to restore the people of Israel to their lost estate as human beings." Likening the British and the Middle East's "twenty eight million Arabs" to Goliath, and Palestine's "eight hundred thousand Jews— besieged and encircled"—to David, Hecht urged the assembled hoodlums to "buy him a stone for his slingshot." Or several stones. Before Cohen kicked off the evening's proceedings, his bodyguard assured Hecht that "each and everybody here has been told exactly how much to give to the cause of the Jewish heroes." There would be, he was promised, "no welchers."

Hecht seemed tickled by Cohen's bullying philanthropic efforts and was clearly fascinated by the dapper Jewish mobster, with whom he somehow identified. "I have always been a sort of pencil-outlaw," he later wrote. "I felt in Mickey a fresh (and happily cock-eyed) point of view against society." But all the tough guys in the world couldn't protect him when in October 1948, the British Cinematograph Exhibitors Association—which represented some thirty-five hundred English movie theaters— finally got around to banning any film on which Hecht's name appeared. It's not clear what took them so long. By now, the British had left Palestine, war raged in the newly declared state of Israel, and Hecht had announced himself done for good with the cause of Hebrew liberation. The various committees disbanded at the end of 1948, when Hecht delivered a final ad- dress at a New York banquet in honor of Begin. Hecht's house- guest in Nyack for a few days, the former Irgun commander was by then head of the right-wing Herut party, whose soon- to-be-elected representatives in the first Knesset would include Bergson and Merlin.

Yet even after all this momentous history had transpired, Hecht's "letter to the terrorists" remained stuck in the collec- tive English craw, and he was still described in news reports of the boycott as the " 'Number one Britain hater' of the United States." Unlike the Hollywood Ten and other blacklisted screen- writers and directors whose work and lives were made intensely difficult during these same years by the House Un-American

Activities Committee and the capitulating studios, Hecht was both happy to shout his controversial political positions from the rooftops—and completely alone in his predicament, the sole target of this particular embargo. As he would note with perplexity, long after the "British had forgiven all the other Jews who had battled them—allowing even Menachem Beigin [*sic*] to publish his memoirs in London—they continued to berate and boycott me as if, God save me, I was busy shelling the coast of Albion with some private cannon."

Hecht claimed with typical swagger that on first hearing news of the ban, he'd been proud. He called it "the best press notice I had ever received—a solid acknowledgment of the work I had been doing with all my might." His sense of satisfaction quickly faded, though, when he arrived on the West Coast, eager as ever to beef up his bank balance, and discovered that he was persona non grata on his old stomping ground. English markets were, it seems, too important to risk on a Ben Hecht script, and the man who had once been the highest-paid screenwriter in Hollywood found himself not only unemployed—but also something of a pariah.

Given his extreme ambivalence about moviemaking in general, this snubbing prompted in him a predictable scramble of feelings. Announcing the "disappearance of the once fabled money maker" whose "vamoosing is like the departure of some pet, say a voracious hippo who has been crowding one out of one's own house," he wrote Rose from Oceanside that "the boycott has finally caught up with me—or put an end to my movie buzzing altogether. . . . Whatever happens, the thought of my bumbling around the major studios and under the guidance of semi terrified nonentities cooking up more movie crap is not an alluring one. I'm grateful for the boycott and the attendant 'dealing me out' for the vanishing of that prospect."

That said, there were bills to pay. Hecht had always been terrible at holding on to what he earned; as easily as money came to him, it went. And with several homes to keep up, as well as a secretary, a household staff of four, and a wife and young daughter to dress, feed, and entertain in style, along with his own none-too-modest tastes—for clothes, cigars, daily visits from his "strongman trainer," Elmore Cole, and the suite he often rented at the Algonquin—he had come to rely on infusions of cash from his regular studio stints, and he couldn't afford to be completely "dealt out." (For all Hecht's financial obliviousness, he seemed to enjoy playing the dual roles of lavish provider and put-upon check-writer, describing in semicomic, almost epic terms the entourage that accompanied him and Rose when they traveled together from Nyack to the West Coast: Lester the driver would transport Elmore, along with the "old ladies," Gertie, Joe, and Hilja, the trusted German- and Finnish-born housekeepers/cooks/servants/cleaners who lived with the Hechts for decades, as well as Googie, the poodle. Six trunks, twenty suitcases, radios and phonograph records, oil paintings, and "favorite window drapes" went by freight, while the family took the train.)

He eventually found screenwriting work—but at a fraction of his old salary, and with various indignities thrown in for good measure. Samuel Goldwyn hired him to do a few anonymous rewrites at fire-sale rates, and Howard Hughes—declaring, "No Englishman is going to tell Howard Hughes whom he can hire"—paid Hecht and Lederer half their standard fee to polish (in fact rewrite almost from scratch) a script that he wound up rejecting. As Lederer later put it in a court deposition that resulted from this messy affair, Hecht had agreed to take far less than usual because "he felt that Mr. Hughes's gesture of defiance toward th[e] boycott constituted a valuable asset that might set a happy example for other major studios." Hughes then deemed "not up to snuff" a second Hecht-Lederer script and deducted a large chunk of their initial payment when they wrote yet another screenplay, for the smart, unsettling alien-invasion picture *The Thing from Another World*—directed by Christian Nyby with major help from Howard Hawks—though all Hughes's big talk came to little: in the final cut, Hecht's name was excised from the credits.

Others tried harder to help. Twentieth Century–Fox's (non-Jewish) Darryl Zanuck was, according to Hecht, "the only studio head who would hire me and use my name . . . [and he] got into a peck of trouble doing it," first putting Hecht and Lederer to work on another script for Hawks. In this return to their shared screwball beginnings—initially called *Darling, I Am Growing Younger*, wisely retitled *Monkey Business*—Cary Grant's Coke bottle–glasses–wearing chemist and Ginger Rogers, as his Betty Crocker-ish wife, gulp an elixir of youth prepared on the sly by a chimpanzee named Esther and then regress, with delight, first to adolescence, then childhood, and almost to diapers. (Perhaps the "temptation of infantilism," as Jacques Rivette described the dark force that lures these ostensibly comic characters backward, appealed in particular to Hecht the six-year-old Jew.) While at around the same time Zanuck conscripted Hecht to write *Whirlpool* and *Where the Sidewalk Ends* for producer-director Otto Preminger, there were limits to what even a determined studio boss could do. When *Whirlpool* was first released in England, its screenplay was attributed to Lester Bartow, Hecht's faithful driver. The suavely WASPy-sounding and entirely fictional "Rex Connor" was named as the writer of *Where the Sidewalk Ends*—though anyone paying attention might have recognized Hecht's stamp on both these brooding psychological thrillers. Tossed off as their scripts may have been, each shows Hecht at his most unapologetically hard-bitten. Preminger's muscular direction—what he himself once called "the style of a man"—was well suited to the coolly hypnotic dramatization of various tropes and types that had obsessed Hecht since the start of his writing life. In *Whirlpool*, the sharp-talking sociopath played by Jose Ferrer is in his own words

"a liar, a swindler, without a touch of . . . human conscience"—
a homicidal variation on the manipulative, verbally dexterous
figure Hecht had rendered repeatedly since *Erik Dorn*. And in
Sidewalk, Dana Andrews plays a police detective, the son of a
crook, who kills a man by accident and—shades of *Crime Without Passion*—winds up digging himself deeper and deeper into
trouble by trying to cover up the crime. Never mind Hecht's
absolutist off-screen notions of heroes and villains in Palestine.
As in so many of his scripts, the usual lines between bad guy and
good—or gangster and district attorney, cop and robber, psychoanalyst and psychopath—are blurred to the point of erasure.

No such ambiguity held when it came to Hecht's own professional predicament. In the minds of Britain's film exhibitors,
he remained quite simply the devil, and little could be done
to convince them otherwise. Bergson applied his old lobbying
skills, offering to send senators Gillette and Malone onto the
senate floor to take up the matter of the ban as he also pestered
various British MPs with regular pleas to end the boycott. Billy
Rose deployed financier and former FDR adviser Bernard Ba-
ruch to do "a little work behind the scenes" on Hecht's behalf.
Despite all their efforts, the official embargo persisted for nearly
four years.

If nothing else, the new chill in the Hollywood air cleared
his mind and his schedule to think of other things. As he worked
on an uncredited revision of *Roman Holiday*, whose script was
originally written by the also-uncredited Dalton Trumbo, blacklisted at the same time for alleged Communism, Hecht mused
to Rose that "most of the social excitement, if not all of it, I had
here was an echo of the success that attended my work, a sort
of hullabaloo raised on the edges of my writing board." Now
such social excitement was a thing of the past, and the compromises the studios demanded and that Hecht had always complained about so noisily were, he claimed, easier for him to
swallow for being off the record. As he put it to Selznick, "Half

my aversion to writing movies is removed if I don't have to see my name on them." Though he didn't hesitate to put his name on the film that would be his last as producer and director, *Actors and Sin*. Written in a week, shot in eight days in October 1951—again with the help of Garmes and Antheil—this independently funded, two-part send-up of both Broadway and Hollywood, based on a couple of his own short stories, seemed meant to serve as mocking payback for the multiple indignities he felt he'd suffered at the hands of producers over the years. Among its cast of cartoonish characters is the pompous, dim-witted studio head J. B. Cobb, who bears more than a passing resemblance to L. B. Mayer, and whose brilliant new screen-writing discovery—author of the "most sophisticated love drama ever filmed"—turns out to be a nine-year-old blonde brat (played by none other than the eight-year-old blonde brat Jenny Hecht, in her acting debut and what one critic characterized, rightly, as "a vastly bizarre performance"—all strange smirks, whined lines, and coy glances at the camera, or perhaps at her mother, right behind it. Rose had by now given herself over to the tireless promotion not just of Ben's career, but also of Jenny's.) As with several of Hecht's other cinematic ventures during this time, the mildly amusing but basically trifling lampoon landed him in more trouble than it may have been worth, as Mayer was enraged and pressured theater owners not to show the film; its distributor, United Artists, fought back in court; and the theater owners countered that they'd canceled the movie's bookings when they realized the picture was "unfair to Hollywood" and that "Mr. Hecht went too far with his satire." As, it seems, did this over-the-top attempt to crush an extremely minor movie, which, for its ostensible venom, registers as little more than playful parody, hardly the harshest its creator had dished out over the years.

While Hecht's legal kerfuffles and pseudonymous scripts kept him busy enough, the simultaneous end of his work for

Directing Jenny

the Irgun and the imposition of the boycott left him hungry for some larger, more meaningful project into which to sink his teeth and his talents. As he explained in an especially candid letter to Rose's psychoanalyst sister, Minna Emch, "Now that the Committee has gone to Palestine to mumble its way through a decade of tiddlywinks, I feel as if Rose, not I, has been deprived of some sort of cohort. Me—" he admitted, "I'm a little relieved not to be involved any more. My indignation against the British is an indignation against illogic and pin headed savagery—which I find in almost all human thought—in all mass thinking—in all politics. My only ambition—I've almost never had any before—is to turn myself into a book—to become a book."

It was, in an odd way, another return to his roots. As early as 1929, in the final issue of Margaret Anderson's *Little Review*, whose contributors constituted an all-star lineup that included everyone from Gertrude Stein to Constantin Brancusi, Ernest Hemingway, and Marianne Moore, Hecht had written, "I am now working on a book called 'A Child of the Century' which will be, when finished, two volumes long and will be sold for $5 and come in a box. I have been occupied for two years by this work which will be peculiarly Jewish. It will be published next year. If I am lucky it will signalize my first appearance as (what the girls used to call) an Artist."

A Child of the Century did not appear then—though over the next few decades mention of various manuscripts with this title bobbed up in vague and passing fashion across his correspondence. But now here he was, with time on his hands and a new sort of perspective, ready again to be recognized as (what he himself used to call) an Artist. On hearing that Hecht had gone back to The Book, Selznick enthused, "It has always seemed to me a really great tragedy that with the whole world waiting for the great American novel, your talent—one of the few that could possibly add impressively to the literature of our country—should be wasted on those Pico Boulevard rewrites. . . . I want so much for the Ben Hecht of Hollywood and of politics to take a good dose of sleeping medicine; and for Ben Hecht, the master novelist, to again triumphantly display his gift."

But Hecht had other—better—ideas. A frank, full, and more or less nonfictional account of his own life and times would be much greater and more jubilantly American than any novel he might stitch from whole cloth, though it had taken him this long to admit as much. At the start of the hefty (654-page) memoir that would become—despite its predictably Hechtian tendency to fudge facts, scramble timelines, and indulge in occasional gusts of defiantly windy philosophizing—without question his finest book, he mused about the delay in getting around to his ideal form and subject: "I was, in my dreams of self, never quite finished with becoming what I hoped to be and, thus, inclined to hold my tongue as unworthy of my future wonders."

He had, however, "decided to put away such convenient humility and accept myself as completed—wonders and all. . . . Obviously, if I keep postponing the task, no book at all will come to pass and the empire I call myself will vanish without its ideal historian to chronicle it."

Published by Simon and Schuster in June 1954, and sold, as predicted, for $5, this peculiarly Jewish reckoning with that empire he called himself, as well as several other empires besides, was, for all its obvious excesses, a word-happy, scrappy tour de force, a book described in the years after Hecht's death as "in its wit and scope probably one of the greatest American literary autobiographies"—though "literary" and "autobiography" somehow make it sound more polite and navel-gazing than it really is. Hecht may have borrowed his title from Alfred de Musset's oh-so European and Romantic *La Confession d'un enfant du siècle* (The confession of a child of the century), but his own book bounces along with a decidedly American brand of propriety-smashing glee—into and out of the basements and backyards of Racine, Chicago's newsrooms and bordellos, Broadway backstages and Hollywood backlots, multiple smoke-filled Committee offices, and his own Nyack kitchen. While he alludes elusively to his multiple affairs—"my adventures with women"—and to what he characterizes as Rose's "courage" and apparently limitless forbearance, describing in the abstract a sort of model wife whose "sturdy belief in him . . . baffles most onlookers and often makes her seem a gullible zany," and who "continu[es] to love him honorably when other women have 'dishonored' him," his memoir is less genuinely confessional than keenly observant. *Child* teems with vivid renderings of tens of dozens of *others*—parents, friends, aunts and uncles, mentors and rivals, heroes, bosses, conspirators, foes. And despite its multiple score-settling riffs on Hollywood moguls, "cringing" American Jews, FDR, and "the Socialist Jews led by Ben-Gurion, the Zionists and the Jewish Agency-ites," whom he lambasts as "timorous" (and who he claims deserve little credit for establishing Israel, which was created by a "handful of Jewish patriots," the Irgun), at its core, the book brims with a molten generosity.

On its initial appearance *Child* was greeted with a typically mixed critical response, though one much warmer than might have been expected, given the antipathy that had surrounded so much of what he'd been up to of late. Most reviewers felt it necessary to fault him for "cheap vulgarity," "coarseness for coarseness sake . . . an amoralism that is not only astounding in itself but is paraded before the world with unchecked pride." (Hecht's unvarnished mention of sex—the fact that he often had it and admitted he liked it—seemed to be what most agitated these critics, though by today's standards, this aspect of the book seems almost quaint in its restraint.) At the same time, they admitted its "brilliance . . . cleverness . . . luminous imagination" and credited him with "superb anecdotes, excellent portrait sketches."

Writing in the *New York Times Book Review*, meanwhile, another adopted literary son of Chicago, thirty-something recent National Book Award winner Saul Bellow, lifted the book and its author to another level, admitting Hecht's place in his own evolution as a writer. As a young man, Bellow and his friends had "combed the second-hand bookstores" for all they could find of his work and, on reading it, were amazed that he "should have conceived of dignifying what we saw about us by writing of it, and that the gloom of Halstead Street, the dismal sights of Back of the Yards and the speech of immigrants should be the materials of art. Something could be made of the very things that baffled or oppressed us, and the chains of today might become the laurels of tomorrow." Turning to the memoir itself, Bellow offered an appreciative assessment of Hecht's strengths and a forgiving reckoning with his weaknesses, accounting handily for both his vigor and his bluster—"His manners are not always nice, but then nice manners do not make interesting autobiographies, and this autobiography has the merit of being intensely interesting."

At the same time, praise flew in from far-flung colleagues and companions, with the novelist William Saroyan scrawling Hecht a note to call it "a hell of a book—preposterously wonderful, properly wild, contradictory, and now and then plain ordinary bad. . . . R[odgers] & H[ammerstein] should make a grand musical of it under its present title & your friend Selznick should make a big movie of it under the title Ben Hecht, writer—they've done inventors, prize-fighters, singers, soldiers, gamblers . . . it's time they got around to writers." Weighing in from the McNeil Island Federal Penitentiary in Washington state, prisoner #22508, Mickey Cohen, wrote in a schoolboy's careful longhand to extol the book as "most wonderfull reading. And if I could of enjoyed it so much with the handicap of needing a dictionary to understand better certain words, and paragraphs of it, I can now well understand why it is a best seller. And the reason for your reknown reputation."

The book did indeed linger some six months on the bestseller list—where it remained lodged several notches beneath Norman Vincent Peale's *The Power of Positive Thinking* and, for part of the time, Hecht's old friend Carl Sandburg's monumental biography of Abraham Lincoln, both of which seemed fitting company for a book that reveled so raucously in the company—lofty and lowly, disreputable and distinguished—its author had spent his life keeping.

Epilogue: The End

"If I had no wit or words
I might weep over what I know."
—*A Child of the Century*

HAVING AT LAST turned himself into a book, Hecht didn't actually cease to *be*, though his last decade was marked by the deaths of many of his friends, and, as his writing of this period mellowed into melancholy, it also swarmed with their ghosts. Working in this increasingly elegiac mode, he seemed aware that he too had begun the final countdown.

Mankiewicz was the first to go, in 1953, at age fifty-six, which was upsetting if not exactly a surprise, since he'd been drinking himself to slow death for as long as Hecht had known him. The chronically soused Bodenheim might have met a similar cirrhotic or uremic end, except that his actual demise came far more violently, when, in February 1954, the sixty-two-year-old poet and the troubled young woman he'd married soon after his wife of many years had died were shot and stabbed to death in a Bowery flophouse. The murderer was one of his new wife's lovers, a schizophrenic dishwasher who defended himself in court by shouting, "I ought to get a medal. I killed two Communists." Bodenheim's death hit Hecht especially hard—both because of its brutality and because of the critical role the poet had played in his own early life. Though it had been years since they'd spent real time in each other's company, Hecht remained loyal, and after all their noisy public feuding had faded and Bodenheim become a genuine physical and emotional wreck, Hecht arranged to send him regular checks, in exchange for poems and prose updates. Signed "Bogie," "Maxwell," or "Friend Bogie," these notes offer, as Hecht put it, "one of the most desperate self-portraits I have ever read." Hecht's archive spills with more than a hundred of these pleas for cash, attention, human warmth, and for all their monotony, each cuts to the quick with its anguished specificity: "The weekly cheque has not yet arrived. I hope I did not irritate you by asking for extra money to save my typewriter." Or: "We are on the verge of getting a dispossess notice and I wonder whether you might not have a job for me on your Nyack estate. Light manual labor would be O.K. with me, if you have nothing else available." Or: "I am sick, and Grace [his wife of decades] has incurable diabetes and cardiac weakness, but in comparison to displaced people in European concentration camps; displaced Jews herded on the island of Cyprus; and slum-dwellers fighting vermin and rats, we are fairly well off, I suppose. Telling yourself that you are relatively well off is a wan antidote for the poisons of a world and ones own physical pain but . . . the spine must not be allowed to break."

For all the misery of Bodenheim's existence, it was precisely his unbroken spine that Hecht so admired. However pitiful in the eyes of others, the poet persisted for him as symbol of a heroic refusal to compromise—and perhaps as a kind of barbed reminder of other paths he himself might have taken, for better or for worse. On hearing the news of the murder from a reporter who called him for comment, a shocked-sounding Hecht wrote Jenny, aged ten, recalling that "when Bogie and I were friends, he was a young man who lived on top of verbal steeples and walked on sidewalks not visible to other citizens. He had no money to eat or buy clothes but he made people seem like paupers when he grinned at them. He was the only poet I ever knew who lived only in the land of poetry and recognized words as the only riches there were."

The next few years brought the deaths of Mencken and Grosz, Antheil and Fowler, though the loss that shook Hecht most deeply was Charlie MacArthur's in 1956. Just sixty when he died, Charlie seemed utterly spent. He had always been a heavy drinker, but the situation worsened precipitously after 1949, when his and Helen Hayes's nineteen-year-old daughter, Mary, died of polio. Then he sank into a state of near-permanent inebriation and, according to Hayes, "set about killing himself." Long before MacArthur conceded to the keen "awareness of death" that Hecht said had always characterized his friend ("He was born without the illusion of permanence. He knew, at the beginning, the road's end"), the onetime partners had been gradually growing apart. MacArthur's fitful work habits and his (or Hayes's) fascination with Hollywood high society and its trappings had taken a toll on the writers' relationship. Even so, the Hecht-MacArthur legend lingered on, long after "the boys" had grown into paunchy, jowly older men with very different tastes, styles, and preoccupations.

Throughout it all, Hecht veered between affection for and frustration with his best friend. In a letter to Rose from the late 1930s, he admitted finding MacArthur "so dull, sad, empty[,] dead and troublesome that I thank God I got rid of him when I did. He would have muffled me for 10 yrs. more hadn't I,"

though in fact they continued to collaborate for at least another decade. (Their final play together was a 1946 flop called,
appropriately, *Swan Song*.) And in another letter from around
the same time as the first, Hecht announced plaintively to Rose
that MacArthur was "as much a part of my life as anything—
except you." It was complicated. From Chicago to Broadway
to Hollywood to Astoria to Nyack, they had lived an entwined
daily existence; both their personal lives and public personae
were inextricably linked, and while it's tempting to describe
them as having been like brothers, their sometimes fruitful,
sometimes painful bond was perhaps more like that of a couple
caught in an intense if not exactly happy marriage. They brought
out the best in each other and they brought out the worst; they
loved and doubted each other as they loved and doubted themselves, and when Hecht described standing to eulogize Mac-
Arthur at his funeral, he admitted, "I felt a bewilderment that
almost silenced me. I wondered which of us was stretched out
in the flower-heaped coffin."

Hecht kept busy during these years with his usual flurry of
disparate projects—a memoir that reckoned with "the improbable life and times" of MacArthur (*Charlie*), a play about Bodenheim (*Winkelburg*), a collection of short stories from across his
career (*A Treasury of Ben Hecht*), a final novel (the rather lurid
sexual thriller *The Sensualists*), another gathering of Chicago
reminiscences (*Gaily, Gaily*), a collection of correspondence
from seven of the talented friends who had predeceased him,
along with his own brief, powerful portraits of each (*Letters from
Bohemia*, published—fittingly—posthumously). After spending
five days in a San Francisco hotel room in early 1954 interviewing the movie star he called "La Belle Bumps and Tears," he
ghostwrote a memoir for Marilyn Monroe—an undertaking
he described to the Doubleday editor who had commissioned
it as "the longest series of log jams I've ever run into."

The situation was especially aggravating because he badly needed the cash he'd been promised, which wasn't forthcoming. Since the boycott, money had become a pressing concern, and the Hechts' back taxes had piled up. Rose had even turned to Selznick with a humiliating request for a loan, which he couldn't manage, though he offered to serve as guarantor at the bank and eventually found Hecht a lucrative TV script to write. ("Such is genius, I suppose," Selznick wrote Rose, "that one can't be a lord of language and at the same time have even an elementary recognition of the awful inevitability of taxes!") Hecht had taken the ghostwriting job thinking it would be quick and relatively easy—and at first everything seemed to go according to plan, as Monroe had been, he said, "100% clinging and cooperative." But then she married Joe DiMaggio and "the picture changed," as the sports icon and her lawyer demanded much tighter control of the text—and when she and DiMaggio split up after just nine months, she was devastated, and refused to comment on the divorce for the book, a draft of which now languished on editor Ken McCormick's desk. Calling the situation "critical," McCormick proposed "shift[ing] this all over into the third person and do[ing] a Ben Hecht biography of Marilyn Monroe. . . . It seems to us that this would give you an elegant chance to write one hell of a book about Hollywood." Hecht preferred to remain anonymous in this context, and meanwhile, his notoriously shady agent, Jacques Chambrun, had secretly sold this ventriloquized version of Monroe's words to a British tabloid which serialized it with neither her nor Hecht's permission, landing the writer in legal trouble. (The book, *My Story*, wasn't published until 1974, long after the deaths of both; it was only in 2000 that Hecht was acknowledged publicly as the author.)

He then took another stab at narrating a life not his own by focusing on a figure much closer to his heart—Mickey Cohen—a biography of whom would, Hecht said, "give . . . me a chance to attack the hypocrisies of society from a more primitive and gaudy point of view than psychologists (except Dostoevski) have usually taken." The two worked together, with Hecht interviewing the gangster in "cars, cafés, bars, anyplace I could get him" and even traveling to La Paz, Mexico, for a more intensive one-on-one session. Hecht drew up multiple drafts of what was taking shape as his own idiosyncratically essayistic first-person account of Cohen's life and crimes; he also wrote a movie treatment based on the mobster's adventures and tried to interest various Hollywood friends—but when it emerged that Cohen had given a lengthy interview on the sly to the *Saturday Evening Post*, Hecht felt the story had been scooped, and scrapped it.

At the same time he continued to crank out the usual heaps of screenplays. While he had always considered his writing for Hollywood a basically mercenary enterprise, he'd also taken a prankster's delight in the slapstick process of collective creation, as well as quiet pride in the best of the movies he'd written. During these years, however, a particularly desultory air hovered over his film work, as he hastily doctored several scripts for Otto Preminger (*The Court Martial of Billy Mitchell*, *The Man with the Golden Arm*); wrote dialogue-to-be-dubbed for the Italian sirens and sailors who populated Mario Camerini's unabashedly shlocky Technicolor *Ulysses*, with Kirk Douglas as a Homeric hero who looks like he might winter in Palm Springs; turned his treacly novella *Miracle in the Rain* into a still more cloying screen parable, starring Jane Wyman and Van Johnson; demanded that his name be removed from a sitcommish Cold War rehash of *Ninotchka* (and his own *Comrade X*), *The Iron Petticoat*, starring Katharine Hepburn as a humorless Soviet jet pilot and Bob Hope as an easygoing American air force captain with official orders to charm her. Dismayed when Hope enlisted his own team of writers to enlarge and make more predictably Hopeful his own role, Hecht took to the pages of the *Hollywood Reporter* to revile the movie as a "mutilated venture," from which Hepburn's "magnificent comic performance [had] been blowtorched." He also dispatched an enraged telegram to John Woolf, one of the heads of the British studio that had coproduced the film, denouncing "YOUR SABOTAGING OF THE IRON PETTICOAT" as "ONE OF THE MOST IMBECILE DEEDS IN MOVIE HISTORY." Hecht traced the studio head's willingness to let Hope dominate back to Woolf's "aversion" to Hecht and his Irgun work: "YOU ARE THE TYPE OF ENGLISH JEW WHO HAS NEVER BEEN OFF HIS HANDS AND KNEES SINCE HE SAW HIS FIRST DUKE." The boycott had been lifted several years earlier, but in Hecht's mind its traces rankled.

Meanwhile, he also lent (or hired out) a hand on several screen adaptations of novels, most notably when, throughout stretches of 1956 and 1957, he holed up in New York, then London, then in a rented villa outside Rome and wrote the script for Selznick's misguided *A Farewell to Arms.* Given Hecht's long-standing contempt for—or was it jealousy of?—Hemingway and the producer's determination to turn the spare antiwar classic into a maudlin romantic vehicle for his wife, Jennifer Jones, the film was probably destined to fail. According to the movie's original director, John Huston, who worked with Hecht on an early version of the script before Selznick's compulsive meddling drove him to quit, the film had been "agony for [Hecht, and] it was certainly a great disappointment to me. . . . David's interference made the already difficult job almost impossible for Ben. Talking to him in Italy, I had the feeling he was now just trying to get out from under—to type the last page, get his money, and go home."

Which may have had less to do with this particular picture than with how he'd been feeling lately about the medium generally. In *A Child of the Century* he describes a walk he said he and Selznick had taken together through the empty streets of Hollywood one dawn in 1951. As they strolled, Hecht wrote,

With Selznick, on location, *A Farewell to Arms*

Selznick declared the movies "over and done with . . . like Egypt . . . full of crumbled pyramids. . . . Hollywood might have become the center of a new human expression if it hadn't been grabbed by a little group of bookkeepers and turned into a junk industry." Selznick himself balked at this account: "I don't recall having said what he quotes me as saying," he insisted, after reading Hecht's memoir. "It could be harmful."

But maybe this too was a kind of ventriloquism. As Hecht

scripted these lines for his old friend, he was really speaking for himself.

Television didn't exert on him the allure the movies had at their most flamboyantly pharaonic, but Hecht did dabble in this new form—dashing off a smattering of teleplays in the early and mid-1950s, and, in February 1958, giving a typically plucky interview to Mike Wallace, who spent much of this entertaining exchange trying to force Hecht to face the apparent hypocrisy of his attitude toward Hollywood, which, for all his debt to it and it to him, he continued to proclaim no more than a stinking trash heap.

More sharply still, Wallace confronted Hecht with the question of his "smiling cynicism" and the compromises he'd made over the years. Had he sold out to "make a buck"? To which Hecht shot back, "Every oil man, every radio commentator, everybody who works sells out, usually sell[s] out more than their minds—they sell out their souls. . . . They usually throw in the sponge when they're about twenty-two or twenty-three and they quit, they become echoes, they echo each other. They're terrified of making any odd remark, even at the dinner table. The American has become in my time one of the most ironed out human beings I've ever seen."

Whatever else he was guilty of, no one could accuse him of such timidity or conformity. And while the network executives were, according to Wallace, "irked" by much of what Hecht had to say during their exchange, he and his producer saw in the onetime newspaperman the makings of a singular TV personality. "Perhaps a regular dose of Ben Hecht, we thought, would awaken the viewing public from what [Hecht] called 'the optical opiate' that television had become." So they signed him on for *The Ben Hecht Show*, which debuted in the 10:50 P.M. slot on September 15, 1958, on New York City's WABC-TV and ran nightly for twenty-two weeks, during which time Hecht managed to interview everyone from Jack Kerouac to Archbishop Makarios of Cyprus to Zsa Zsa Gabor, the poet John Ciardi, and cartoonist Al Capp, as well as old friends like Billy Rose, Peter Bergson, S. J. Perelman, and Otto Preminger, and a variety of unfamous people engaged in exotic professions—a medium, a stripper, an executioner.

As the show moved from these free-flowing conversations to Hecht's crusty responses to viewers' letters and on to his own memory-laced monologues (on subjects that included the Chicago of his youth, the Holocaust, censorship, Charlie Chaplin, and prostitution), his tone modulated between prickly and sleepy- or distracted-sounding. Was he going a little soft in older age? Perhaps, but "soft" is a relative term, and by the down-pillow standards of the day's television, Hecht's personality seemed a dangerously rusty nail. Although initially that figured as a selling point—the show's theme song was "Mack the Knife," by his old friend and collaborator Kurt Weill—over the months, the skittish network executives grew more and more concerned with his frank manner and provocative choice of guests. They refused to allow him to host both Alger Hiss and Norman Mailer (to discuss his essay "The White Negro"), and canceled the broadcast on the night he scheduled a live discussion with a group of Bowery bums. Then—they had probably been looking for just such an excuse—the day after Hecht interviewed Salvador Dalí, and the Spanish surrealist unblinkingly described a marvelous new kind of orgasm, they pulled the plug, and *The Ben Hecht Show* flickered off for good.

But Hecht didn't need a TV network to help him put on a show. In his last years he threw himself into staging an audacious grand finale to the audacious production his whole life had been. This came in the form of two ambitious prose works that were hardly the only projects he took on during this period, though they seem to have absorbed much of his attention.

While quite distinct from each other, both were polemics designed to provoke, both pivoted around dramatic courtroom confrontations, and both wrangled with questions at once urgent and eternal—of justice and mercy, power and powerlessness, compromise and revenge. And both were, as Hecht proved in writing them still to be, obsessed with anti-Semites and Jews.

For all his passionate earlier involvement with the Bergsonites and the Irgun, Hecht had, by his own admission, detached himself from the state of Israel after it had come into being, never once visiting, "even as a tripper." (At times he claimed indignantly that he would never set foot there as long as David Ben-Gurion's Mapai party remained in power, while Merlin claimed that Hecht was officially unwelcome in the country. It's more believable, though, to think that he'd simply burned through his fascination and turned his attention to the next thing.) Furthermore, he had "kept intact" his "ignorance of the progress of the Israeli Government, its various unions, money collection agencies and economic plans. But . . . suddenly," sometime in the 1950s, "distant echoes" of what was known as "the Kastner case" had, he said, reached him and "stunned" him into action. After seeking the help of an Israeli lawyer named Shmuel Tamir, a former Irgun commander who, in Hecht's words, "turned accuser of Israel," Hecht wrote *Perfidy* —or *Perfidy in Israel*, as it was originally titled—"in anger and astonishment."

Or so he described the genesis of the sensational 1961 book in an unpublished draft of its preface. In fact, it's clear from the archive that it was the charismatic Jerusalem native Tamir himself who did the seeking—writing Hecht from Tel Aviv as early as August 1955 to praise him lavishly for *A Child of the Century* and for being "the first who told the whole world the naked truth about the universal conspiracy concerning the extermination of the Jewish people on the one hand, and about the real forces who acted for and against the revolutionary upheaval which brought about the creation of the State of Israel." (By those who acted for that upheaval, he meant the Revisionists and the Irgun, whom Hecht had credited with having "terrorized the British out of Palestine.")

"With the same penetrating force," Tamir continued, "you were the first who has managed to show and to define how petty, how ugly, how dangerous and how unscrupulous was the clique who for fifteen years had gone about with the 'gallows in their hearts.'" By whom he meant Ben-Gurion, Chaim Weizmann, and the rest of the Labor Zionist leadership—whom Hecht had accused in his memoir of having willfully sacrificed most of Europe's Jews as they urged on to Palestine "only the best of Jewish youth . . . only people of education." Had he, Tamir wondered, ever heard of the Kastner case? As he sent along a pile of clippings about the recent Jerusalem trial, he reminded Hecht that in the farewell speech the writer had given at the Waldorf Astoria in late 1948—welcoming Begin to America as he bid farewell to Bergson and Merlin—he'd declared his retirement as Irgun propagandist, though, as Tamir remembered it, "Then you paused for a while, raised your head and added: 'But boys, if ever there be a great cause again—my typewriter is still there!'" Tamir knew the way to the aging rabble-rouser's heart: "My dear Hecht, the cause is here again. A great cause. A cause which calls for your typewriter. I am now in the midst of a savage fight against the 'Ancient Regime' of this country, though I am not a member of any political party." He was, he said, "all alone—against the whole government and all it stands for."

The thirty-two-year-old Tamir also knew a few things about putting on a show—or, as it happened, a show trial. The affair that would come to be known by the name of Kastner (or Kasztner) and that would eventually unseat an Israeli prime minister and shake the fledgling state to its very foundations—arguably making way for much of the political turmoil that has defined Israel since, as it represented the first meaningful challenge to the country's then all-powerful reigning party, Mapai—began as something much quieter. This was a libel suit brought by the State of Israel against an elderly, yarmulke-wearing Hungarian refugee named Malchiel Gruenwald, who owned a modest Jerusalem hotel but spent much of his time wandering the city's cafés distributing poorly mimeographed screeds against various public officials, especially those connected to Mapai. Generally considered a crank, Gruenwald was always making outrageous claims in these exclamation-point-strewn diatribes, which usually garnered little response. But it seems he crossed some invisible line when in August 1952 he began circulating a particularly emphatic assault on the Transylvania-born journalist and Mapai functionary Israel (Rudolf or Rezsö) Kastner, who, while living in Budapest during the war and serving as the head of the local Zionist rescue committee, had negotiated with Adolf Eichmann and an SS officer named Kurt Becher to trade ten thousand trucks for a million Jewish lives. (The deal fell through for various reasons.)

At the same time, Kastner—who was known to enjoy power and hobnobbing with powerful people—had also made a deal with Becher to secure a train that would carry 1,684 Jews to safety in Switzerland. To Kastner's mind, this act rendered him a hero, while according to Gruenwald's more than mildly hysterical account, the great savior had in fact made a point of selecting as the train's passengers several dozen members of his own family as well as the elite of his hometown, who constituted nearly a quarter of the train's passengers and who paid or arranged for others to pay a ransom to guarantee their places—suitcases filled with cash, jewels, and gold, to be handed over to Becher. In exchange for the rescue of his own people, Kastner had, claimed Gruenwald, agreed to remain silent about the imminent deportations of hundreds of thousands of other Hungarian Jews, who were then sent placidly to be slaughtered. Gruenwald also charged that after the war Kastner had trav-

eled to Nuremberg, "like a thief in the night" to serve as a character witness for Becher—that "murderer-thief who exploited
our brothers in Hungary and sucked their blood!"—so saving
him from the gallows. In his tightly typed six-page rant, Gruenwald called Kastner "an indirect murderer of my dear brothers," which made him a collaborator, the only crime punishable
in Israel by death: "My nostrils itch with the stench of a corpse!
This will be the finest of funerals! Dr. Rudolf Kastner must be
liquidated!"

Because Kastner worked as a spokesman for the Ministry
of Commerce and Industry, the attorney general felt compelled
to bring suit on his behalf. And while Tamir's lawyerly mandate
was ostensibly to defend Gruenwald against the libel charge,
he understood right away that the case stood for something
much larger than the allegations lodged against one sad-sack
pamphleteer. For Tamir, a direct line existed between the apparent collaboration of Kastner with the Nazis and what he
deemed the pre-1948 collaboration of Ben-Gurion and company with the British in Palestine. As Kastner had been willing
to forfeit the lives of so many Jews in order to save those closest
to him, so the Mandate-era Zionist leadership had performed a
coldly Darwinian sort of calculus in determining who should
be allowed into Palestine and who kept out by British quotas—
that is, who would live and who would die. In 1937, Weizmann
had famously declared that the youth of Europe must be saved
while "the old ones will pass, they will bear their fate or they will
not. They are dust, economic and moral dust in a cruel world."
As Tamir saw it, such apparent indifference to the destiny of
the Jewish masses and such toadying to the British Colonial
Office (whose immigration policies Weizmann seemed to be
endorsing with this statement) amounted to nothing less than
intent to kill. And now the government's determination to protect Kastner sent up a huge red flag. As Hecht would write in
Perfidy, describing in the present tense Tamir's thinking before

he agreed to lift the heavy legal and political load the case represented, "Kastner, Greenwald [*sic*] are actually of minor importance. . . . It is the Government of Israel that asks for battle—and the whole hierarchy of the new State."

Eager to wage that battle himself, Tamir expertly choreographed a theatrical trial during which he ratcheted the stakes higher and higher, turning the courtroom proceedings into a major national spectacle. After a grueling nine months, the enterprising young lawyer got just what he wanted: not only did the judge acquit Gruenwald of all but one count—for which he was fined a single, symbolic lira—he pronounced a thundering verdict on Kastner (who hadn't technically even been on trial). Kastner had, wrote the judge, "sold his soul to the devil." And when, in the stormy days that followed, Prime Minister Moshe Sharett made clear that his government would lodge an appeal with the Supreme Court "in order to allow Kastner to defend himself," two no-confidence motions were promptly filed. In the midst of the uproar, Sharett submitted his resignation and dissolved the government. The results of the elections that followed marked a startling change of political key. Mapai lost five Knesset seats, while Herut—the party of Irgun hero Menachem Begin—rose from eight to fifteen.

The saga hardly ended there. Kastner was assassinated in 1957, and some nine months later the Israeli Supreme Court cleared him of all Gruenwald's accusations, except the charge concerning his testimony on Becher's behalf, with one of the justices writing in his forgiving opinion of the "danger in attempting to objectively judge the behavior of 'dramatis personae' from the past—including the not so distant past. . . . One tends to fail to place oneself in their situation." But Kastner's exoneration wasn't the last word either, as the affair marked a kind of beginning—a critical shift in the country's nascent sense of self. The case was, as a Tel Aviv journalist described it then, "not only . . . a fight for historical truth . . . [but] a struggle for the shape of the Israeli regime in the future." That assessment would prove more than headline-grabbing hyperbole when in 1977, for the first time in the country's history, the right wing took control of the government. Begin became prime minister, and Tamir the minister of justice.

But that was still years off, and as Tamir had come out firing, so now did Ben Hecht. *Perfidy* is nothing if not a flamboyant rhetorical shoot 'em up, with Hecht blasting his way straight into the middle of an enormously complicated conversation and—without ever slowing to take in the painful complexity of the matter at hand—letting out a massive, defiant barrage. Far from subtle, the book is alive with the rage that had always animated him when it came to the Holocaust—though what's odd here, and what ultimately renders *Perfidy* more revealing as biographical curio than convincing historical argument, is that Hecht's fury was directed squarely at the heart of contemporary Israel and its rulers—subjects about which he'd been quick to confess he knew very little and cared even less. But urged on by Tamir and still nursing a severe anti–Jewish Establishment grudge from his years with the Bergsonites, Hecht let it rip, writing a vividly, unabashedly one-sided and wildly reductive account of the entire affair. Announcing on page 2 that his book has three heroes—Gruenwald, Tamir, and the judge who rendered the initial verdict—he then gets down to naming his villains: Kastner, the attorney general, and the real bad guys, Weizmann, Sharett, and Ben-Gurion. According to Hecht, "the politicized princes of Jerusalem" did "not think of Jews dying in Europe, but of government thriving in Palestine, and they thriving with it."

The verbal bravado was vintage Hecht, while the particulars of the trial and its background—the legal exhibits, as it were—came mostly from Tamir. Although the book is dedicated to the lawyer, and his praises are operatically sung throughout, and though Tamir himself credited Hecht entirely with the book's

authorship—in a telegram he predicted that "YOUR MONUMEN-
TAL BOOK WILL GO INTO HISTORY AS THE GREATEST JACCUSE OF
MODERN TIMES"—copious correspondence between the two re-
veals the major role the attorney played in its composition. Feeding Hecht court transcripts, newspaper clippings, documents,
translations, timelines, Tamir fact-checked him repeatedly and
even wrote the detailed and most un-Hechtian "Reference
Notes" that appear at the back of the book, many of which come
straight from Hebrew, a language of which Hecht was unapologetically ignorant. The lawyer traveled to London and to
Nyack to work through the manuscript in person with Hecht,
and they tussled over the "good number of inaccuracies" that
Tamir had identified in the text and that he considered "dangerous . . . enough to expose the book—and all it stands for—
to an indefensible attack." Hecht, for his part, accused Tamir of
being "frightened" by insisting on these fine points, which the
writer saw as excessively legalistic and liable to "dull the style
and fog up the meaning of a sentence or paragraph." Tamir was
hurt at being called a coward, but Hecht soothed him by explaining that "my calling you 'frightened' was chiefly due to the
fact that I too was frightened at the time, and still am. [This
was July 1961, five months before the book came out and shortly
after the start of that far more famous Jerusalem Holocaust
trial, Adolf Eichmann's.] I have always been apprehensive about
the uproar that Perfidy will unloose. My feeling has been,
however that there is no way to avoid or outwit such an uproar.
It will come regardless of how deftly legal the book is. Just as
you will take a clobbering in your Israel, I shall receive a similar
whacking in the United States." Hecht credited Tamir with
having "invented" the book and, bizarrely in the context of this
most self-righteously Jewish of disquisitions, described him as
"a Santa Claus who came down my chimney with the greatest
gift I ever received."

That was one of the milder ironies surrounding his attitude

toward this book and the radioactive material it contained. Not only was Hecht the utterly American Jew taking up and arguing Tamir's aggressively Israeli position as he built his case using all the details the lawyer had supplied him, *Perfidy* is, despite its withering criticism of Israel's rulers ("the Ben-Gurion Kleagles," he called them), a full-frontal attack on what the Revisionists deemed a "diasporic" way of thinking. The wheeling and dealing of Kastner and Ben-Gurion, their pragmatism, their sometimes cutthroat survival instincts, their willingness to negotiate with powerful (even contemptible) non-Jews, were, from this Jabotinsky-ite point of view, highly suspect, the product of a fatally exilic outlook. Resistance, revolt, even martyrdom—these were the only legitimate strategies available to the new Jew, the real man.

But Ben Hecht, no martyr he, knew a thing or two about compromise—and even if he'd recently bristled on live national television at the mere suggestion that he'd sold out, he had in fact spent his life making deals, hustling, opting for the actual over the ideal, improvising with wile, *collaborating*, if you will, in the more positive sense of that term. Much of his best work had, in fact, been the product of collaboration—and while whipping off a Hollywood script with an old pal like Lederer or MacArthur, or doctoring a screenplay for Hawks or Hitchcock, Selznick or Zanuck hardly entailed the same crushing ethical concessions as did bargaining for Jewish lives with Nazis during wartime, Hecht himself certainly never aspired to the purity it seems he demanded of the players in this wrenching life-and-death drama. That paradox seemed to land squarely in his blind spot. For all its trademark energy and acidic wit, the book shows Hecht farther out of his element and less self-aware than ever. Not only was he plain wrong about much of this history, he seemed not to know that there were a great many things that he didn't know. The book's bluster is unnerving even for Hecht, since he often seems to be arguing for argument's sake—as a matter of stubborn habit rather than raw necessity.

There was, too, something grotesque about the way he leaned back in his Nyack lawn chair and accused the likes of Weizmann and Ben-Gurion—even Rudolf Kastner—of not really caring about the fate of the Jews. Hecht was absolutely right to insist that the leaders of the Jewish state were no more virtuous than other leaders. "What happened to Jews when they became Jewish politicians?" he asked ominously in the opening pages—and answered with the book-long blitz that followed. He was also perfectly justified in fulminating about the dark fact that "the government of the Jews could not save the Jews." The book's flatly comic-strip-styled demonization of Israel's founders, though, did a serious disservice to the profoundly round characters these men really were, and to the almost impossible choices they'd faced. Fallible, admirable, arrogant, energetic, at once boldly forward-looking and terribly short-sighted, they were, in other words, not so different from himself.

While *Perfidy* would become something of a cult classic on the Jewish right (among its admirers was Revisionist rabbi Louis Newman, who'd once savaged Hecht from the pulpit for that "atrocious malignment of the Jews" that he considered *A Jew in Love*), Hecht was correct in predicting that many critics would whack him for it. Soon after its publication in December 1961, he was accused of "crude distortions of history" and the book called "evil . . . in every sense of the word." Liberal American Zionists denounced it for obvious reasons, though more conservative readers decried it as well. One pious polemicist even felt compelled to write and publish in both English and Yiddish "The Man and His 'Perfidy,'" a 103-page "rejoinder" to this "Vitriolic Attack Upon the Government and Leaders of

Israel," in which the writer described the book as "a continuation of Auschwitz. In it, as at Auschwitz, living Jews are flayed; in it, Jews are burned. In it, the guilt is taken from the non-Jewish world and placed upon the Jews themselves. . . . No Jew dare say 'I am blameless.' But neither may any Jew say 'You, you are to blame.' The final judgment must rest with Him who is the ultimate Judge."

These "brick-bats," as Hecht called them, seemed almost the reaction he'd hoped for—"New enemies pop up like weeds under my feet. Clippings arrive full of angrier and more preposterous denunciations," he wrote Tamir. "And all this gives me a feeling that you and I did well. PERFIDY seems to act like all effective medical injections—they cure by shock."

And as always he had moved on to other matters. "I feel I have reached an age," he mused to Selznick in early 1964, "where I should slow down and break my old habit of working on three things at once. And I intend such reforms in my life"— though not quite yet. Besides writing a script drawn from Ian Fleming's *Casino Royale*, "in which James Bond single-handedly shuts down a score of brothels and stamps vice out in the whole of Europe," he had "finally got a glimpse of backing for my musical, 'Chicago.'" This was to be based on *Underworld*. (Neither the finished, farcical 1967 *Casino Royale* nor the brassy Kander and Ebb song and dance show *Chicago* has much if anything to do with what it seems Hecht was planning.) He was at the same time deeply immersed in a final nonfiction project.

Though this manuscript would remain incomplete at his death, even in its somewhat ragged state, it stands as a striking companion piece to the Kastner volume and a tantalizing coda to his life's work. If *Perfidy* damns boldly and simplistically— using swagger and scorn to indict a whole gallery of those he deemed villains—this last work is a far more meandering, almost cud-chewing attempt to redeem from villainy one of the most misunderstood, richly complicated, and troubling Jewish

characters of all time. Part rambling literary treatise, part can-
tankerous memoir, part earnest religious-historical tract, part
playfully speculative biographical sketch, the work-in-progress
might also be read as an attempt to redeem another often misunderstood, richly complicated, and troubling Jewish character, none other than Ben Hecht.

In *Shylock, My Brother,* Hecht makes his case for Shakespeare's stiff-necked Venetian moneylender as "one of the few
heroic Jews in classic literature, perhaps the only one." Although the figure has often been dismissed as the height of anti-
Semitic caricature, for Hecht, "branding Shylock a villain is
part of the fear thinking of the Jews." Shylock's vengeful and
unwavering demand for a pound of the loan-defaulting merchant Antonio's flesh makes him to Hecht's mind "a valiant vin-
dicator of Jewish grievance" and "one of the first unfrightened
Jewish voices to speak out to Christendom." Here, as in all his
explicitly "Jewish" works, Hecht defines Jewishness in mostly
negative or reactive terms, in response to anti-Semitism. (Attempting to describe his own "persistent Jewishness," he explains, "I am the end product . . . of an infinitude of disasters, a
multitude of humiliations. In some deep way, my sanity consists
of loyalty to these misfortunes.") And once again, defiance and
intransigence are virtues to be celebrated, while a willingness to
compromise is anathema, the surest sign of weak Jewish knees.

But Shylock is hardly a strapping Irgun fighter, armed with
Bren gun and grenade. If anything, he's the very ghetto-dwelling,
ducat-lending, kashrut-keeping, Bible-citing embodiment of the
diaspora Jew at whom Hecht had been known lately to sneer,
though the character's strong personality trumps such stereotypes. "Shylock survives because of his humanness," writes
Hecht. "His cartoon drifts out of the play. His truth—his vigor,
pride, and refusal to be crushed by his detractors, remain." Furthermore, "he answered his abusers with wit rather than a wail
of pain." Which also sounds vaguely familiar—yet as Hecht

was busy identifying with Shylock, he also made clear the blood bond he felt with the character's celebrated creator, going so far as to riff on a myth he "would like to believe is true"—that Shakespeare himself was secretly Jewish. Living a sort of double life in ostensibly Judenrein Elizabethan England, this marrano-esque version of the Bard meant (or so Hecht fantasized) to stir sympathy for the Jews by summoning Shylock onto the Globe's stage in all his angry, funny, flawed, and vital glory, as a kind of perverse exemplar. This Shylock speaks for Shakespeare, who also speaks for Hecht: "If you tickle us, do we not laugh? If you poison us, do we not die? And if you wrong us, shall we not re-venge?" It might as well have been his own motto.

That said, trawling this manuscript for some final word about Hecht and the Jews is at best a precarious business. Not only are the extant drafts patchwork, stop-start affairs, the proj-ect began as a much dryer, grayer essay by his old Irgun buddy Samuel Merlin, which Hecht started to copyedit, and then—inspired or infected by what Merlin had written—subsumed into his own longer and more imaginatively capacious work. And this in turn seemed almost a collaboration with Rose, who had always been intimately involved with his prose and with his Jewish activism, but who seems to have played an especially significant role in the composition of *Shylock*. She herself wrote to Merlin in early 1963, explaining sheepishly what they were up to: "You handed Ben a wonderful manuscript which we soon saw as a powerful platform—a kind of neutral U.N. place from which to survey once more the journey of the Jewish soul in Time to which we three are pledged in this life." Although she predicted Merlin would be "very angry," in fact he approved wholeheartedly—declaring himself "spellbound" by the manu-script . . . which continued to evolve even after Hecht's death, as Rose revised it heavily—except that now he wasn't around to speak up or fight back, and the text has a muddled quality as a result, caught somewhere between their sensibilities and styles. Brainy, bitter Rose was a gifted if cramped and overself-conscious stylist, and after she published two novels, in 1927 and 1933, her own freestanding prose-writing career had more or less faded out. As fanatically devoted as she was to Hecht's reputation, and then to his memory—for years she kept a "stink book," a dossier of his critics ("I will be avenged," she wrote of them, apparently in earnest), and, in her extreme grief right after he died, threatened to burn down the Nyack house where they'd spent all those decades together—the manuscript suffers from what feels like both her long-simmering resentment of all he'd put her through, and her anguished refusal to let him go. Though she continued to work on the text for years—"writing or editing, or whatever it is I'm doing"—consulting (and clashing with) Merlin and various editors, it never emerged as a book.

If nothing else, though, *Shylock, My Brother* makes plain that until the very end, Hecht continued to circle restlessly around the question of where the word *Jew* belonged in his kaleidoscopic sense of self. Rose, for her part, instinctively placed it at the heart of his being when, on the morning of April 18, 1964, a Saturday, she found him slouched over an open copy of e. e. cummings's *The Enormous Room*, having suffered a heart attack. She tried to coax him back to life, failed, and on realizing that he was gone, began speaking to him "tender words" in broken Yiddish. "Except for a lullaby I used to sing to Jenny," she'd later remember, "I had never spoken of love in the mother tongue. I felt those words would reach his soul."

After his funeral—a jam-packed affair at Temple Rodeph Sholom on the Upper West Side, presided over by the once-Hecht-bashing Rabbi Newman, and with eulogies by George Jessel, Luther Adler, Bergson, Tamir, and Begin, Hecht did the unthinkable, and finally came to rest.

Yet even that final repose wasn't a given. The files of the Jabotinsky Archive in Tel Aviv contain a letter dated 2003, written in Hebrew by several old Irgun stalwarts and addressed to then–prime minister Ariel Sharon, demanding the recognition of Ben Hecht's "great contribution to the Jewish people and the State of Israel" and the immediate reinternment of his and Rose's bones in Jerusalem. It's not clear why this exhumation and reburial didn't take place, though it seems much more fitting that Hecht—who to the end never once set foot in Israel—remains in the plot he and Rose had chosen and where she and Jenny would eventually join him, alongside Charlie and Helen and their children. This placid green Nyack hill overlooking the Hudson isn't exactly a kosher Jewish burial site, but more like a spot for a long, lazy picnic, a place he could linger with people he loved, and a view of the water, flowing.

IN WRITING THIS BOOK, I've drawn extensively from the Ben
Hecht Papers, Midwest Collection, Newberry Library, Chicago.
Hecht's copious correspondence, drafts of his work, speeches,
photographs, clippings, financial and legal documents, and various
objects—date books and passports, pipes and letter openers, his
first Oscar—make up much of this remarkable archive, as does a
great deal of material produced by Rose Caylor Hecht and Jenny
Hecht. Also at the Newberry, the Ben Hecht Filmscript Collection,
the Sherwood Anderson Papers, and the William MacAdams–Ben
Hecht Research Papers were important sources of information.

For further details about Hecht's work with the various Bergsonite committees, I relied on the files of the Palestine Statehood
Committee, held at Yale University; the archive of the American
League for a Free Palestine, American Jewish Historical Society,
the Center for Jewish History, New York; and the Jabotinsky Archive, Tel Aviv. The papers of Kurt Weill and Lotte Lenya, also
at Yale, provided additional material about the pageants on which

Weill and Hecht worked together. However unreliable a narrator Hecht could be, his own books—especially the memoiristic *A Child of the Century* (New York, 1954), *Charlie: The Improbable Life and Times of Charles MacArthur* (New York, 1957), *A Guide for the Bedevilled* (New York, 1944), *Gaily, Gaily* (Garden City, NY, 1963), and *Letters from Bohemia* (Garden City, NY, 1964), as well as the occasionally autobiographical *A Thousand and One Afternoons in Chicago* (Chicago, 1922) and *1,001 Afternoons in New York* (New York, 1941)—have been essential resources in reconstructing his life and times, as has *The Ben Hecht Show: Impolitic Observations from the Freest Thinker of 1950s Television* (Jefferson, NC, 1993). I'm grateful to that book's editor, Bret Primack, for sharing with me the recordings of many of those shows, which allowed me to hear Hecht's own sixty-five-year-old voice in all its warmth, good humor, and crankiness. Joan and Robert Franklin's transcribed 1959 interview with Hecht, part of the Popular Arts Project of Columbia University's Center for Oral History Research, was a useful source, as was a talk about Hecht and MacArthur, delivered by Helen Hayes at the Newberry Library in October 1980. The archives of various newspapers—the *New York Times*, the *New York Herald Tribune*, and *PM*, in particular—were critical to my research.

I've also been glad for the presence of several previous books about Hecht. William MacAdams's *Ben Hecht: The Man Behind the Legend* (New York, 1990) provides an excellent filmography and bibliography, while Doug Fetherling's *The Five Lives of Ben Hecht* (Toronto, 1977) offers elegant commentary on Hecht's evolution and is especially astute about his literary work. Jeffrey Brown Martin's *Ben Hecht: Hollywood Screenwriter* (Ann Arbor, 1985) is a solid reckoning with his scripts, while the highly enterprising researcher Florice Whyte Kovan has established a website and publishing house, Snickersnee Press, devoted solely to unearthing and publishing hard-to-find Hechtiana. Though it's not concerned solely with Hecht, Richard Corliss's *Talking Pictures: Screenwriters in the American Cinema* (Woodstock, NY, 1974) remains an essential resource on Hecht and his hyperverbal Hollywood peers.

Additional sources for individual chapters appear below.

Prologue

Assessments of Hecht come from Jean-Luc Godard, *Jean-Luc Godard: Interviews*, ed. David Sterritt (Jackson, MS, 1998); Menachem Begin, quoted in "Ben Hecht Is Buried in Nyack Near Charles MacArthur Grave," *New York Times*, April 22, 1964; Mike Wallace, "The Mike Wallace Interview," February 15, 1958, Harry Ransom Center Archive; Burton Rascoe, quoting Pound, in James Branch Cabell, *Between Friends: Letters of James Branch Cabell and Others*, ed. Padriac Colum and Margaret Freeman Cabell (New York, 1962); Pauline Kael, *For Keeps* (New York, 1994); Kael, "The Current Cinema," *New Yorker*, December 20, 1969; Corliss, *Talking Pictures*; H. L. Mencken, *My Life as Author and Editor*, ed. Jonathan Yardley (New York, 1993); Bosley Crowther, "Home Is the Hunter, Home from the Hills," *New York Times*, September 19, 1937; George Jessel, *So Help Me* (New York, 1943). Hecht's account of the "surprising number of me's" appears in *A Treasury of Ben Hecht* (New York, 1959); his bordello musings are from *Child*, and his American-Jewish comments come from *Guide*.

1. The Root

This chapter weaves material from *Child* with excerpts from Hecht's adolescent diary and his letters to Rose Caylor from the 1920s. Information about Racine's history comes from Gerald L. Karwowski, *Racine* (Charleston, SC, 2007), and George D. Fennell, *Racine* (Charleston, SC, 2014), as well as *The Comet*, the Racine High School yearbook. I have given the date of Hecht's birth as 1893, since this is what appears on his own passports and multiple census records. Various sources—including his tombstone and the Library of Congress Name Authority File—list 1894. Self-styled chameleon that Hecht was, it's no great surprise that his official documents are inconsistent in other odd ways: his eyes magically morph from blue to gray to hazel over the course of different passports and draft registration cards.

2. The News

Besides Hecht's own memoirs and correspondence, details of the Chicago newspaper and literary worlds of this period are derived from Vincent Starrett, *Born in a Bookshop: Chapters from the Chicago Renaissance* (Norman, OK, 1965); Harry Hansen, *Midwest Portraits* (New York, 1923); Robert M. Crundan, *American Salons: Encounters with European Modernism, 1885–1917* (Oxford, 1993); Burton Rascoe, *Before I Forget* (New York, 1937); Henry Justin Smith, *Deadlines: Being the Quaint, the Amusing, the Tragic Memoirs of a News-Room* (Chicago, 1922); Walter Rideout, *Sherwood Anderson: A Writer in America*, vol. 1 (Madison, WI, 2006); *Sherwood Anderson's Memoirs: A Critical Edition*, ed. Ray Lewis White (Chapel Hill, 1969); Edward Thomas De Voe, *"A Soul in Gaudy Tatters": A Critical Biography of Maxwell Bodenheim* (Ph.D. diss., Pennsylvania State University, 1957). The "genteely WASPy commentator" is Albert Parry, in *Garrets and Pretenders: A History of Bohemianism in America* (New York, 1933). Hecht's article about Rosenfeld is "Yiddish Poet Sees Jews' Future in U.S.," *Chicago Daily Journal*, December 29, 1913. "Sketches for Cartoon of Ben Hecht" by Carl Sandburg (2018) printed by arrangement with John Steichen, Paula Steichen Polega, and the Barbara Hogenson Agency. All rights reserved. For more information about Carl Sandburg visit www.nps.gov/carl.

Marie Armstrong Essipoff's anonymously published *My First Husband, by His First Wife* (New York, 1932), offers her version of their courtship and marriage. Margaret Anderson, *My Thirty Years' War* (New York, 1930), tells the story of the *Little Review*, whose 1914–15 issues I've drawn on here, as I've also gathered material from the *Smart Set* of approximately the same period. Mencken's words about Pound come from *My Life*, while Pound's take on Hecht's stories appears in *Pound/The Little Review: The Letters of Ezra Pound to Margaret Anderson: The Little Review Correspondence*, ed. Thomas L. Scott, Melvin J. Friedman (New York, 1988).

3. The World

Norman Mailer's quip about Hecht appears in *Marilyn: The Classic* (New York, 1973). The various versions of Hecht's momentous first night in Berlin turn up in *Child* and *Letters*. In *My First Husband*, Marie Armstrong offers yet another contradictory account of what happened that night. She describes arriving at the hotel and settling in happily: "The bed was warm, the Rhine wines soothing, the bath room sufficiently American and [Ben] near me." Grosz's version appears in The *Autobiography of George Grosz: A Small Yes and a Big No*, trans. Arnold J. Pomerans (London, 1982).

Hecht's dispatches and letters from Berlin are part of his Newberry papers. His initial articles about the massacre were published in the *Chicago Daily News*, March 15 and 17, 1919; he describes the Dada evening in both *Guide* and *Letters*, and Grosz recounts it differently in *A Small Yes*. For more about the night's performance, see Peter Jelavich, *Berlin Cabaret* (Cambridge, MA, 1993), and on the contradictory nature of the accounts, see Matthew Biro, *The Dada Cyborg: Visions of the New Human in Weimar Berlin* (Minneapolis, 2009).

The Chicago section of this chapter relies on *The Letters of Carl Sandburg*, ed. Herbert Mitgang (New York, 1968); Hansen, *Midwest Portraits*; Henry Justin Smith, Preface, *A Thousand and One Afternoons in Chicago* (Chicago, 1922) and Bill Savage's introduction to the reprint edition (Chicago, 2009); Dale Kramer, *Chicago Renaissance: The Literary Life in the Midwest, 1900–1930* (New York, 1966); Rose Caylor, *The Woman on the Balcony* (New York, 1927); and the extant issues of the *Chicago Literary Times*. Algren's words come from his introduction to the reprint edition of *Erik Dorn* (Chicago, 1963). Details of Rose's college years are drawn from her University of Chicago transcript; *University Debaters' Annual*, vol. 4 (New York, 1918); and the *University of Chicago Magazine*, vol. 10, 1917.

4. The Times

Hecht's *Charlie*, *Child*, *Guide*, and *Letters* form the backbone here. Additional sources: Alexander Woollcott, "The Young Monk of Siberia," from *The Portable Woollcott* (New York, 1946); Stuart Silverstein's introduction to *Not Much Fun: The Lost Poems of Dorothy Parker* (New York, 1996); Marion Meade, *Dorothy Parker: What Fresh Hell Is This?* (New York, 1987); Helen Hayes MacArthur and John D. MacArthur, forewords, *The Stage Works of Charles MacArthur* (Tallahassee, 1974); George W. Hilton, *The Front Page: From Theater to Reality* (Hanover, NH, 2002); Richard Meryman, *Mank: The Wit, World, and Life of Herman Mankiewicz* (New York, 1978); Helen Hayes, with Sandford Dody, *On Reflection: An Autobiography* (New York, 1968); Jhan Robbins, *Front Page Marriage: Helen Hayes and Charles MacArthur* (New York, 1982); Tom Dardis, *Firebrand: The Life of Horace Liveright* (New York, 1995); Walker Gilmer, *Horace Liveright: Publisher of the Twenties* (New York, 1970); Bennett A. Cerf, "Horace Liveright: An Obituary—Unedited," *Publishers' Weekly*, October 7, 1933.

5. The Screen

The telegram's contents appear in *Child*, and the chapter draws from all Hecht's autobiographical work, as well as MacAdams's *Ben Hecht* and Corliss's *Talking Pictures*. Further details about Hecht and Hollywood derive from Pauline Kael, *The Citizen Kane Book: Raising Kane* (New York, 1971); Meryman, *Mank*; Anita Loos, *A Girl Like I* (New York, 1966); David Thomson, *Showman: The Life of David O. Selznick* (New York, 1992); Josef von Sternberg, *Fun in a Chinese Laundry* (New York, 1965); Andrew Sarris, *The American Cinema: Directors and Directions, 1929–1968* (New York, 1968); John Lee Mahin interview by Todd McCarthy and Joseph McBride, *Backstory: Interviews with Screenwriters of Hollywood's Golden Age*, ed. Pat McGilligan (Berkeley, 1986); Todd McCarthy, *Howard Hawks: The Grey Fox of Hollywood* (New York, 1997); Joseph McBride, *Hawks on Hawks* (Lexington, KY, 2013); Robin Wood, *Howard Hawks* (London, 1983); Max Wilk, *Schmucks with Underwoods: Conversations with Hollywood's Classic Screenwriters* (New York, 2004); Jerome Lawrence, *Actor: The Life and Times of Paul Muni* (New York, 1974); Thomas Schatz, *The Genius of the System: Hollywood Filmmaking in the Studio Era* (New York, 1988); Ian Hamilton,

Writers in Hollywood, 1915–1951 (New York, 1990); Fred Lawrence Guiles, *Hanging on in Paradise* (New York, 1975). Hecht's original story for *Underworld* is printed in full in the Criterion Collection supplementary material to *3 Silent Classics by Josef von Sternberg*, as is an excellent essay about the film, "Dreamland," by Geoffrey O'Brien. Further quotations are culled from *The Low Down*; Ben Hecht, "The Screen Whipping Post," *Screenland*, February 1924; and articles in *Variety, Film Daily, Motion Picture News*, and *Moving Picture World*. The estimate of an average screenwriter's salary comes from Larry Ceplair and Steven Englund, *The Inquisition in Hollywood: Politics in the Film Community, 1930–60* (Berkeley, 1983). The Motion Picture Producers and Distributors of America's 1927 list of "Don'ts and Be Carefuls"—their litany of what was frowned on or prohibited onscreen, which formed the basis for the Production Code—appears in *Hollywood's America: Twentieth-Century America through Film*, ed. Steven Mintz and Randy W. Roberts (West Sussex, 2010).

6. The Rogues

Donald Friede's memories of publishing *A Jew in Love* appear in *The Mechanical Angel* (New York, 1948). On the Astoria experiment: Lee Garmes interview in Charles Higham, *Hollywood Cameramen: Sources of Light* (Bloomington, IN, 1970); Guiles, *Hanging on in Paradise*; Richard Koszarski, *Hollywood on the Hudson: Film and Television in New York from Griffith to Sarnoff* (New Brunswick, NJ, 2008); Noël Coward, *The Letters of Noël Coward*, ed. Barry Day (New York, 2007); Noël Coward, *Future Indefinite* (London, 1954); George Antheil, *Bad Boy of Music* (Garden City, NY, 1945); and multiple *New York Times* articles. Peter Hecht is quoted in a letter to Steven Fuller (a.k.a. William MacAdams) in the MacAdams papers at the Newberry.

7. The Jews

Details about the making of *Foreign Correspondent* are drawn from the correspondence between Joseph Breen and Will Hays,

History of Cinema, Hollywood, and the Production Code: Selected Files from the Motion Picture Association of America Production Code Administration Collection; James Naremore, "The Windmills of War," in the Criterion Collection DVD; Donald Spoto, *The Dark Side of Genius: The Life of Alfred Hitchcock* (New York, 1983). The account of and quotes from *Fun to Be Free* are drawn from the commemorative program, and "Freedom Rally Thrills 17,000," *New York Times*, October 6, 1941. Other sources for this chapter: Neal Gabler, *An Empire of Their Own: How the Jews Invented Hollywood* (New York: 1988); Paul Milkman, *PM: A New Deal in Journalism, 1940–1948* (New Brunswick, NJ, 1997); and David Nasaw, *The Patriarch: The Remarkable Life and Turbulent Times of Joseph P. Kennedy* (New York, 2012).

Biographical details about Peter Bergson and the specifics of Hecht's first encounters with him are drawn from Louis Rapoport, *Shake Heaven and Earth: Peter Bergson and the Struggle to Rescue the Jews of Europe* (Jerusalem, 1999); David S. Wyman and Rafael Medoff, *A Race Against Death: Peter Bergson, America, and the Holocaust* (New York, 2002); Judith Tydor Baumel, *The "Bergson Boys" and the Origins of Contemporary Zionist Militancy* (Syracuse, NY, 2005); Rebecca Kook, "Hillel Kook: Revisionism and Rescue," in *Struggle and Survival in Palestine/Israel*, ed. Mark LeVine and Gershon Shafir (Berkeley, 2012); Yitshaq Ben-Ami, *Years of Wrath, Days of Glory: Memoirs from the Irgun* (New York, 1982); Samuel Merlin, *Millions of Jews to Rescue: A Bergson Group Leader's Account of the Campaign to Save Jews from the Holocaust*, ed. Rafael Medoff (Washington, DC, 2011); Alex Rafaeli, *Dream and Action: The Story of My Life* (Jerusalem, 1993); Monty Noam Penkower, "In Dramatic Dissent: The Bergson Boys," *American Jewish History* 70, no. 3 (1981); Eran Kaplan, "A Rebel with a Cause: Hillel Kook, Begin, and Jabotinsky's Ideological Legacy," *Israel Studies* 10, no. 3 (2005).

8. The Cry

In addition to the sources cited for the previous chapter and the various archival collections listed above, I've relied on the interviews conducted by Claude Lanzmann with Peter Bergson and

Samuel Merlin, 1978, available through the United States Holocaust Memorial Museum; David S. Wyman, *The Abandonment of the Jews: America and the Holocaust, 1941–1945* (New York, 1984); Deborah E. Lipstadt, *Beyond Belief: The American Press and the Coming of the Holocaust, 1933–1945* (New York, 1986); Rafael Medoff, *Militant Zionism in America: The Rise and Impact of the Jabotinsky Movement in the United States, 1926–1948* (Tuscaloosa, 2002); *The Personal Letters of Stephen Wise*, ed. Justine Wise Polier and James Waterman Wise (Boston, 1956); Melvin Urofsky, *A Voice That Spoke for Justice: The Life and Times of Stephen S. Wise* (Albany, 1982); A. James Rudin, *Pillar of Fire: A Biography of Rabbi Stephen S. Wise* (Lubbock, 2015); *Speak Low (When You Speak Love): The Letters of Kurt Weill and Lotte Lenya*, ed. and trans. Lys Symonette and Kim H. Kowalke (Berkeley, 1996). Particulars of the Bergsonites' ads and articles about the various pageants are culled from the *New York Times, New York Herald Tribune, Los Angeles Times, Philadelphia Inquirer,* and *PM.* Quotations from the State Department and British Foreign Office are drawn from Rapoport, *Shake.*

9. The Flag

Sources for this chapter not previously listed are Perkins's letters to Hecht from the Newberry; *Editor to Author: The Letters of Maxwell E. Perkins,* sel. and ed. John Hall Wheelock (New York, 1950); Marlon Brando, with Robert Lindsey, *Songs My Mother Taught Me* (New York, 1994); Atay Citron, "Ben Hecht's Pageant-Drama: *A Flag Is Born,*" in *Staging the Holocaust: The Shoah in Drama and Performance,* ed. Claude Schumacher (Cambridge, 1998); Robert O'Donnell Nicolai, "I Ran Britain's Palestine Blockade," *Pageant,* August 1947; "My Uncle Abraham Reports," *Chicago Sun,* November 10, 1943 (published in multiple papers over this month).

10. The Child

This chapter also draws from: François Truffaut, with Helen G. Scott, *Hitchcock* (New York, 1983); Andy Warhol's interview with Hitchcock in *Alfred Hitchcock: Interviews,* ed. Sidney Gottlieb (Jackson, MS, 2003); Bill Krohn, *Hitchcock at Work* (London, 2000); Leonard J. Leff, *Hitchcock and Selznick: The Rich and Strange Collaboration of Alfred Hitchcock and David O. Selznick in Hollywood* (Berkeley, 1987); Sidney Gottlieb, "The Unknown Hitchcock: Watchtower over Tomorrow," *Hitchcock Annual*, 1996–97; Meyer Levin, *In Search: An Autobiography* (Paris, 1950); Frank Mankiewicz, with Joel Swerdlow, *So As I Was Saying . . .: My Somewhat Eventful Life* (New York, 2016); email to the author, from Frank Mankiewicz, October 28, 2011; Mickey Cohen, *In My Own Words: The Underworld Autobiography of Michael Mickey Cohen as Told to John Peer Nugent* (Englewood Cliffs, NJ, 1975); Jacques Rivette, "The Genius of Howard Hawks," in *Cahiers du Cinéma: The 1950s*, ed. Jim Hillier (Cambridge, MA, 1985); Peter Bogdanovich, *Who the Devil Made It: Conversations with Legendary Film Directors* (New York, 1997); Hecht, "Farewell My Bluebell," *Little Review*, May 1929. The assessment of *Child* as "one of the greatest American literary autobiographies" is Fetherling's. The reviews quoted are from the *New York Times* and the *Jewish Exponent*. Saul Bellow's review is "The 1,001 Afternoons of Ben Hecht," *New York Times*, June 13, 1954.

Epilogue

Nonarchival material about the final stage of Hecht's life comes from John Huston, *An Open Book* (New York, 1980); "The Mike Wallace Interview"; Wallace's foreword to *The Ben Hecht Show*; Helen Hayes, with Katherine Hatch, *My Life in Three Acts* (New York, 1990).

Background on the Kastner trial comes from Yechiam Weitz, *The Man Who Was Murdered Twice: The Life, Trial, and Death of Israel Kasztner*, trans. Chaya Naor (Jerusalem, 2011); Tom Segev, *The Seventh Million: The Israelis and the Holocaust*, trans. Haim Watzman (New York, 1991); Shalom Rosenfeld, *Criminal File 124: The Gruenwald-Kastner Trial* [Hebrew] (Tel Aviv, 1955); Yehuda Bauer, *Jews for Sale? Nazi-Jewish Negotiations, 1933–1945* (New Haven, 1994); Shmuel Tamir, *Son of This Land* [Hebrew] (Lod, 2002); Yechiam Weitz, "The Herut Movement and the Kasztner Trial,"

Holocaust and Genocide Studies 8, no. 3 (1994); Yechiam Weitz, "The Holocaust on Trial: The Impact of the Kasztner and Eichmann Trials on Israeli Society," *Israel Studies* 1, no. 2 (1996). Weizmann's words appear in "On the Report of the Palestine Commission," in *The Zionist Idea*, ed. Arthur Hertzberg (Garden City, NY, 1959). The journalist who described the case as a "struggle for the shape of the Israeli regime in the future" was Uri Avnery. The reviews of *Perfidy* quoted here are by Homer Bigart, "A Matter of Personalities," *New York Times*, January 28, 1962, and Shlomo Katz, "Ben Hecht's *Kampf*," *Midstream* 8, no. 1 (1962). Other notable reviews include Lucy S. Dawidowicz, "Ben Hecht's 'Perfidy,'" *Commentary* 33, no. 3 (1962), and Marie Syrkin, "Perfidy and Stale Venom," *Jewish Frontier* 29, no. 1 (1962). The pious polemicist was Chaim Lieberman, *The Man and His 'Perfidy'* (New York, 1964).

THANKS

BEN HECHT GOT around and kept very busy. Chasing after him took some doing, but welcome help in tracking down his many movies, books, and far-flung footprints came from Jeanine Basinger, Carolyn Cohen, John Stuart Gordon, Ken Gross, Benjamin Hett, Gerry Karwowski, Becky Kook, Nancy Kuhl, Gabriel Levin, Mimi Muray Levitt, Howard Mandelbaum, the late Frank Mankiewicz, Rafael Medoff, Larry Miller, Zina Miller, Eric Monder, Lisa Moore, Bret Primack, Marta Renzi, Lori Styler, Katie Trumpener, John W. Waxman, Eliot Weinberger, and Daniel Wolff. Joe Florentino and Megan Mangum have again worked their behind-the-scenes magic in various ways. Many moons and movies ago, Ruth Kern planted a seed that would eventually sprout into this book, and I'm obliged to her still.

Martha Briggs, Alison Hinderliter, and the rest of the staff at the Newberry Library have been an archival hound's dream to work with. Michael Kerbel and Brian Meacham were extremely generous with the contents of the Yale Film Studies Center, which played a critical role in my research. I was assisted greatly by the archivists and librarians at the various institutions listed in the Sources section, and I've also been aided in various ways by exacting people at the Harry Ransom Center at the University of Texas, the Menachem Begin Heritage Center, the David S. Wyman Institute for Holocaust Studies, the United States Holocaust Memorial Museum, the George Eastman Museum, the registrar's office at the University of Chicago, and the Beinecke Library.

For commenting on various parts of the book and urging me on throughout its research and writing, a thousand and one afternoons' worth of thanks to Lisa Cohen, Judy Heiblum, Corey Robin, and Nathan Thrall. I'm especially grateful to Jeanne Bloom, Mark Kamine, Phillip Lopate, John Sayles, and Robert Schine, whose expert questions about the whole manuscript helped me revise and refine. Noah Isenberg's keen reader's report was also a huge boost. Miriam Altshuler has been her usual canny and encouraging self, while at Yale University Press, Heather Gold has patiently ushered the book through the intricacies of production, as have numerous gifted others. For his good humor, tact, wisdom, and eagle eye, Dan Heaton deserves not just my appreciation, but the copy-editing equivalent of an Oscar. I owe Ileene Smith yet another bouquet of thanks for her determination to make things happen, her unflappability, and her enthusiasm.

Finally, Peter Cole always reads my books-in-progress as he reads me—better than I read myself.

PHOTO CREDITS

JEWISH LIVES is a prizewinning series of interpretative biography designed to explore the many facets of Jewish identity. Individual volumes illuminate the imprint of Jewish figures upon literature, religion, philosophy, politics, cultural and economic life, and the arts and sciences. Subjects are paired with authors to elicit lively, deeply informed books that explore the range and depth of the Jewish experience from antiquity to the present.

Jewish Lives is a partnership of Yale University Press and the Leon D. Black Foundation.

Ileene Smith is editorial director.
Anita Shapira and Steven J. Zipperstein are series editors.

Primo Levi: The Matter of a Life, by Berel Lang
Groucho Marx: The Comedy of Existence, by Lee Siegel
Menasseh ben Israel: Rabbi of Amsterdam, by Steven Nadler
Moses Mendelssohn: Sage of Modernity, by Shmuel Feiner
Harvey Milk: His Lives and Death, by Lillian Faderman
Moses: A Human Life, by Avivah Zornberg
Proust: The Search, by Benjamin Taylor
Yitzhak Rabin: Soldier, Leader, Statesman, by Itamar Rabinovich
Walter Rathenau: Weimar's Fallen Statesman, by Shulamit Volkov
Jerome Robbins: A Life in Dance, by Wendy Lesser
Julius Rosenwald: Repairing the World, by Hasia R. Diner
Mark Rothko: Toward the Light in the Chapel,
    by Annie Cohen-Solal
Gershom Scholem: Master of the Kabbalah, by David Biale
Solomon: The Lure of Wisdom, by Steven Weitzman
Steven Spielberg: A Life in Films, by Molly Haskell
Barbra Streisand: Redefining Beauty, Femininity, and Power,
    by Neal Gabler
Leon Trotsky: A Revolutionary's Life, by Joshua Rubenstein
Warner Bros: The Making of an American Movie Studio,
    by David Thomson

FORTHCOMING TITLES INCLUDE:

Hannah Arendt, by Peter Gordon
Judah Benjamin, by James Traub
Irving Berlin, by James Kaplan
Franz Boas, by Noga Arikha
Mel Brooks, by Jeremy Dauber
Bob Dylan, by Ron Rosenbaum
Elijah, by Daniel Matt
Betty Friedan, by Rachel Shteir